SOUTH YEMEN

PROFILES • NATIONS OF THE
CONTEMPORARY MIDDLE EAST
Bernard Reich and David E. Long, Series Editors

Also of Interest

SOUTH YEMEN

A Marxist Republic in Arabia

Robert W. Stookey

Westview Press • Boulder, Colorado

Croom Helm • London, England

Profiles/Nations of the Contemporary Middle East

Copyright © 1982 by Westview Press, Inc.

Published in 1982 in the United States of America by
    Westview Press, Inc.
    5500 Central Avenue
    Boulder, Colorado 80301
    Frederick A. Praeger, President and Publisher

Published in 1982 in Great Britain by
    Croom Helm Ltd.
    2-10 St. John's Road
    London SW11

Library of Congress Catalog Card Number: 82-1934
ISBN (U.S.) 0-86531-024-6
ISBN (U.K.) 0-7099-2356-2

Printed and bound in the United States of America

Contents

Illustrations

MAPS

TABLES

PHOTOGRAPHS

(The photograph section follows page 58)

Preface

In October 1963 a group of youthful Yemeni guerrillas, second-echelon leaders of the National Liberation Front (NLF), gathered in secret to discuss the state of their campaign against the British imperial presence in South Yemen and against the South Arabian Federation, which was formed under British guidance and intended to satisfy Arab nationalist demands for an end to colonial rule as well as to secure the tenure of the vital British military base at Aden, then still under construction. The meeting concluded with the public proclamation of the NLF's determination to pursue independent action to evict the colonialists by armed force, an event today commemorated as the National Day of the People's Democratic Republic of Yemen (PDRY). The necessity of violence seemed to disappear eighteen months later, when the British government announced its intention of terminating its imperial role east of Suez within a few years. The NLF nevertheless fought on, not only against the British, but also against the Front for the Liberation of Occupied South Yemen (FLOSY), formed on Egyptian inspiration with the aim of uniting all elements of South Yemeni society against the colonial regime. FLOSY's top leaders were men of international standing who had effectively mobilized general Arab and world opinion against colonial rule in their country and who had realistic hopes of succeeding to power through negotiation with Britain. But the NLF defeated FLOSY's paramilitary formations even before the British withdrew under fire in November 1967, leaving the NLF in undisputed command of the field.

This scenario departs from the conventional pattern of the loosening of ties between an imperial power and a dependent territory. The struggle for independence has more commonly been waged by a broad coalition of nationalist elements, while debate over the restructuring of the independent society and government is deferred until the colonialists have departed. South Yemen's case contrasts wildly with that of the small Arab states of the Persian Gulf, also under British protection until recently. They received the gift of independence almost reluctantly and preserved their traditional governing institutions virtually intact, whereas the traditional South Yemeni rulers' authority had collapsed even before independence. New leaders promptly proceeded to shape socialist institutions with hardly a single root in the country's past and adopted a course in external affairs in which the mystique of Arab nationalism and solidarity seemed to take second place to the advancement of world revolution.

The attempt to explain why the PDRY has embarked on such an unexpected path is among the major concerns of this book. As South Yemen is certainly among the least known of the new countries, an effort has also been made to provide a cogent outline of its venerable and turbulent history and a succinct description of its geography, culture, natural resources, and economy. It is the author's hope that the book will fill the need for a balanced general introduction to the country and its people.

As the work is designed for the general reader rather than the area or linguistic specialist, no rigorous system of transliteration has been used for Arabic words and names. The variety of renderings of the same term from one Western writer on the region to another adds up to utter chaos. Where a given spelling can be expected to be encountered with reasonable frequency in the Western press, it has usually been adopted. Diacritical marks, meaningless to those unfamiliar with Arabic, have been avoided except where necessary to avoid confusion between two or more names or words. Internal consistency has been the primary concern.

The author wishes to express his gratitude to the Permanent Mission of the People's Democratic Republic of Yemen at the United Nations for graciously providing a number of essential documents. Thanks are due also to the Center for Middle Eastern Studies, the University of Texas at Austin, for its support and assistance in many ways, including meeting the cartographic costs. A particular debt is acknowledged to Sir Kennedy Trevaskis, both for his insight into the political evolution of South Yemen and for his kind permission to quote from *Shades of Amber*. The illustrations in this book, finally, are in great majority the work of the author's friend of many years standing, Helen B. Eilts, who generously made available the collection of photographs she took during her residence in Aden and travels throughout the former Protectorates.

R. W. S.

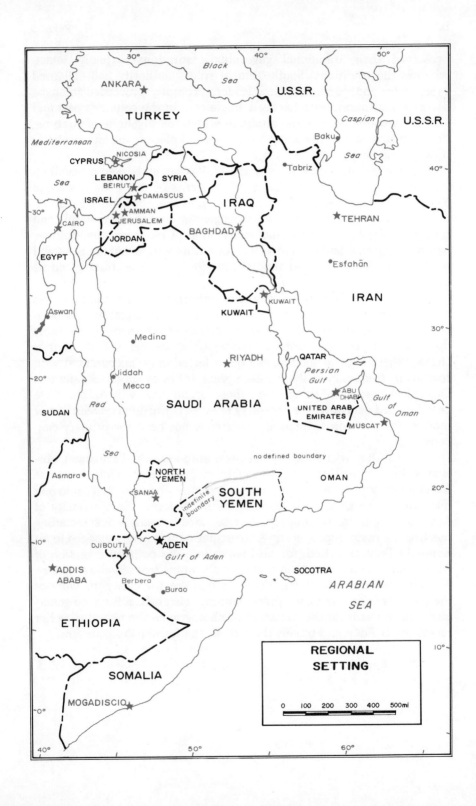

REGIONAL
SETTING

0   100   200   300   400   500mi

1

The Land and the People

South Yemen occupies a wedge-shaped territory at the southwest corner of the Arabian Peninsula, with its apex at the Bab al-Mandab, the strait separating the Red Sea and the Indian Ocean. It also owns the waterless island of Perim, within the strait, and Socotra, a large, semidesert island in the Arabian Sea. The present government claims a total land area of 208,106 square kilometers (80,345 square miles); as the country's borders with North Yemen and Saudi Arabia, in the southern reaches of the Empty Quarter, have never been fully demarcated, this figure must be regarded as an approximation. A distinctive combination of topographical and climatic characteristics sets limits on the abundance and nature of flora and fauna the land can support and consequently on the scope of human activity.

The dominant South Arabian terrain feature is the mountain chain of varying altitude that parallels the entire Red Sea littoral of the Arabian Peninsula from the Gulf of Aqaba south to the Bab al-Mandab, then bends northeastward along the Gulf of Aden and the Arabian Sea to terminate at Ras Musandam at the mouth of the Persian Gulf. Generally speaking, a coastal plain (Tihama) varying in breadth from several kilometers to more than sixty rises to a chain of foothills with mean elevation of a few hundred meters. North of an adjacent plateau the terrain slopes steeply upward to the main ranges of mountains (whose ridges are locally called *kur*: "camel saddle") whose peaks rise to two thousand meters or more and whose northward versant inclines gradually into the sandy wastes of the Empty Quarter. Geological formations are typically volcanic and relatively recent. The highlands are composed largely of metamorphic rocks, limestone and sedimentary material being rather scarce. Where the granitic surface is exposed, it is burned nearly black by the blazing sun. The mean daily temperature at the coast is 26°C (79°F) in winter and 32°C (90°F) in summer; the upper and lower extremes increase markedly with elevation as one moves inland.

The country's meager rainfall is governed by the Indian Ocean monsoons. In spring, the southerly winds precipitate a modicum of

1

moisture on the coastal plain and increasing amounts at the higher eleva-
tions. Thus, Aden receives an annual average of 30 millimeters (1.18
inches) while in the uplands precipitation may reach 600 millimeters
(23.62 inches) or more in a favorable year. The monsoon rains are highly
variable, and the region's history is marked by recurrent droughts, often
extending over several consecutive years.

The bulk of the country's rain falls on terrain too broken and rocky
for extensive cultivation and it comes commonly in brief, torrential
showers. These facts imply that agricultural development sufficient to
sustain a concentrated population requires a special combination of factors. A significant expanse of fertile, relatively level land must be at
hand, and this occurs only in a few favored parts of the coastal plain or,
rarely, on the inland plateaus. This must coincide either with a surface
watercourse (wadi) concentrating the runoff from a substantial area or
with a subsurface structure providing an ample and renewable source of
groundwater that can be brought to the surface for irrigation. The
technology, finally, must be present to construct and maintain networks
of irrigation channels, impoundments or diversion works, wells, and
water-lifting devices. Three major areas meeting these requisites receive
a substantial proportion of their water from the highlands of North
Yemen: Wadi Tiban and Wadi Bana in the Second Governorate and
Wadi Bayhan at the western extremity of the Fourth Governorate. The
spectacular rift of Wadi Hadramawt, in the Fifth Governorate, together
with its several major tributaries, drains a sufficiently extensive area on
the northern slopes of the mountains to support substantial cultivation.
On the coastal plain and at the higher levels of the plateaus, foothills, and
mountains, natural vegetation is adequate to support a scattered
nomadic population of herdsmen who, in years of exceptionally high
precipitation, may also plant and harvest an occasional small crop of
cereal grains.

Such an ill-favored land can, of course, support only sparse fauna,
and South Yemen's is typical of desert and semidesert regions. Water-
fowl, both indigenous and migratory, are relatively abundant in coastal
and marshy areas, including ducks, flamingos, snipes, pelicans, and
various species of heron. Storks are seasonal sojourners. Game birds are
found in small numbers, notably bustard, doves, and pigeons in the
uplands. Hill partridge, sand grouse, crows, and shrikes are rather common, as is the vulture. Songbirds include several warblers and the desert
lark. The ostrich and the panther disappeared early in the present century, as did the desert oryx. Ibex are still present at the higher altitudes.
Some predators—notably the fox and the hyena—persist, as well as rab-
bits, hares, hyrax, the small Arabian gazelle, and occasional troops of ba-

boons. Reptiles are represented by a variety of snakes–cobra, horned viper, puff-adder, and whipsnake–and the monitor and smaller lizards.

Although the coastal plain behind Aden was relatively well wooded in 1839, it was rapidly denuded of trees to satisfy the fuel requirements of the British garrison and the growing port and is now almost entirely without trees. Elsewhere, desert shrubs and trees hold their own: mimosa, tamarisk, camelthorn, and the myrrh shrub. A species of palmetto grows in the rare swampy spots. Grass grows only briefly after showers, whether at the coast, on the plateau, or high in the mountains. The nomadic peoples of South Yemen must thus rely upon browsers–camels and goats–capable of assimilating leaves and twigs, while sheep and cows must be kept close to sources of cultivated fodder.

THE PEOPLE

In broad terms, the people of South Yemen mostly consider themselves to be descendants of Qahtan (the Joktan of the Book of Genesis), the reputed ancestor of the Southern Arabs, as opposed to the Northern Arabs, who regard Adnan as their ancestor. The native stock, however, has been considerably diversified by many centuries of intimate, if intermittent, contact with other peoples. Adnani Arab immigrants settled in various parts of the country beginning in the tenth century and became a distinct religious and scholarly class. East African slaves imported at various periods were absorbed into the population. In large numbers, South Yemenis emigrated temporarily to India, East Asia, Africa, and Hijaz (the Islamic holy land, now a province of Saudi Arabia), intermarrying with the host peoples and thus adding further ethnic elements to the South Yemeni population. The intrusive strains were assimilated most typically in the larger towns. In the more isolated countryside, the indigenous South Yemeni type–wiry, of small stature, and of swarthy complexion–was little altered.

The Arabic language is universally spoken. Like other Arab countries, South Yemen has its own colloquial dialects, not fully intelligible to Arabic speakers from distant regions. It is distinguished by some lexicographical survivals from ancient South Arabic and by terms borrowed from Urdu and other Asian tongues during the British occupation, notably words related to innovative crafts and techniques. The everyday patois is, of course, not written or taught in the schools. The language used in instruction is the classical Arabic of the Koran in the modern, simplified adaptation used throughout the Arab world in formal discourse, broadcasting, and publications. This "standard" Arabic is intelligible even to illiterate South Yemenis–a fact that became politically important in the 1950s, when radio propaganda from Cairo and other Arab nationalist capitals contributed powerfully to arousing the Yemeni masses against the British occupation. Notwithstanding the preponderance of Arabic, English is often used as a language of instruction, particularly in scientific and technological subjects.

THE SOCIAL STRUCTURE

Although the current regime has effected fundamental changes in South Yemeni society, and it is as yet unclear which features of the old order will ultimately survive, examination of the traditional social structure provides a useful perspective in addition to its obvious historical interest. The social patterns existing at the time of the British penetration had certain salient features of great antiquity and others of more recent origin. There were differences among the various districts, and unifying political institutions were virtually absent, but some characteristics were shared throughout the region.

Save in the modern city of Aden, solidarity among agnatic kinship groups was everywhere the binding social factor. This tended to promote cohesion among groups claiming descent from a common eponymous ancestor. At the same time, it set groups apart one from another in unstable relationships of chronic enmity, interdependence, clientship, or intermittent cooperation for specific purposes. It furthermore inhibited mobility among the various strata of society. The preferred pattern of marriage was within the kinship group. Infrequently, a man might take a wife from a social stratum inferior to his own; no woman, on the other hand, was given in marriage to a man of lower social position than that of her own family. As marriage contracts commonly included a substantial dowry settled on the bride by the groom's family, endogamy had the effect of conserving wealth within the kinship group. Economic roles rigorously followed birth, and this helped to reinforce a hierarchy of social classes based upon relative nobility of lineage, of which the religious criterion was one important aspect.

Occupying the center of the social spectrum were the tribesmen, whose crucial role rested on their monopoly of armed force. Although the tribes' unchallenged claim to descent from a single prestigious ancestor, Qahtan, helped to ensure them a respected niche in the social order, it did not foster unity and solidarity among them. Instead, the operative principle was kinship with the local leaders who emerged in the fifteenth century and later, when centralized government declined in South Yemen and ancient patterns of intertribal relations reasserted themselves. Whether settled or nomadic, each tribe claimed ownership of a particular territory, sometimes of fluctuating extent, and defended it fiercely against intruders.

Within clans and tribal sections, local disputes were arbitrated according to systems of customary law by headmen usually elected from recognized families. Their authority, never entirely unquestioned, varied widely in scope and seldom extended to the power to speak for the entire group with outsiders. Dispersal of authority reached the extreme in the Subayhi region, a desert area of about 775 square kilometers (299 square miles) between Lahej and the Bab al-Mandab with a population of perhaps 20,000, where a decision of consequence by a tribal section might require the formal assent of a dozen leading men to become operative. Competition was intense for control of the quite limited productive land. Hostility between a given clan and its neighbors became chronic, often aggravated by protracted blood feuds arising from offenses against the norms of tribal "honor," such as the compromise of a woman's chastity or aspersions cast upon a man's moral qualities or those of his tribe. In the early 1930s, insecurity of life in Wadi Hadramawt reached the point where some people had not set foot outside their houses for two decades, while others had dug long trenches to permit safe passage between their residences and their cultivated fields. At the same period, chronic feuds among tribes to the west made it impossible for European visitors to travel overland between the Wadi and Aden. Elaborate codes had been formulated to mitigate the loss of life and economic disruption resulting from intertribal strife, but these often failed to fulfill their intended purpose.

No tribe, however, could live entirely to itself. Weapons, ammunition, various craft products, and often food commodities had to be procured in exchange for what the tribesmen could produce in surplus. Traffic along the traditional trade routes from North Yemen or Wadi Hadramawt to the sea, furthermore, could not be totally and permanently halted. Specific mechanisms to deal with these problems had appeared over the centuries and were incorporated into the social fabric.

Each tribe asserted its right to permit or forbid passage by outsiders through its territory. It became customary for the traveler or the trader to engage a member of the tribe through whose land he passed to ensure the security of his life and property. This custom came to encompass the levy of tolls on merchandise in transit. The caravan traffic provided the opportunity for some camel-raising tribesmen to become freight carriers themselves—one of the few occupations not considered demeaning to this warrior class.

Long predating the Islamic era, the institution of the sacred enclave (called *hawta* in South Yemen) served a stabilizing function in South Yemen as in other parts of Arabia. The prestigious model, of course, is the *haram* at Mecca that, before Muhammad, had been a center of worship of pagan gods. Administered by the Prophet's clan, Quraysh, its immunity from violence was strictly respected by the warring tribes, who gathered there at specific seasons to perform religious rites, conduct trade, and negotiate over their disputes, in which Quraysh served as mediators. Such enclaves existed in South Yemen, and after the area's conversion to Islam they passed into the custody of shaikhs (*mashayikh*),[1] often converted members of the existing custodial families, revered because of their learning in the disciplines of the new religion. Often a new *hawta* grew up around the tomb of a respected religious figure, built in the beehive shape and whitewashed—a distinctive feature of the South Yemeni landscape. His descendants, to whom his spiritual virtue was assumed to be transmitted, retained custody of the enclave, and some attained substantial influence as mediators among the nearby tribes.

Many of the indigenous *mashayikh*, however, were superseded by sayyids, descendants of the Prophet Muhammad through his daughter Fatima, who married his cousin Ali bin Abi Talib. Sayyids migrated to South Yemen beginning in the mid-tenth century A.D. and developed into an aristocracy of considerable wealth and influence throughout the country. They were commonly acknowledged to have inherited the Prophet's discernment (*baraka*) in matters of the faith, and their claim to high status was bolstered by meticulously maintained records of their ancestry, which they could trace without a break to the Prophet, and beyond him to Adnan. They held a monopoly of formal education until late in the British protectorate era. Many emigrated temporarily to South and Southeast Asia, East Africa, Hijaz, and elsewhere, acquiring wealth as religious leaders or merchants as well as political horizons that enhanced their influence upon their return home. As they avoided bearing arms, their power rested on their moral sway over the tribes; sayyid families often entered into durable agreements with certain tribes by which the sayyids' security was ensured in recompense for their religious, peacemaking, and political services. During the anarchic period in Hadramawt before "Ingrams's peace" of the late 1930s, sayyid clans governed some towns as virtually independent entities. In Bayhan a family of sharifs[2] established a ruling dynasty in cordial treaty relations with Britain.

Although important as political brokers throughout South Yemen, the sayyids did not hold a monopoly of the mediating and aggregating functions. When the British established themselves in Aden, they conceived of the hinterland as divided among tribes living in well-defined territories, whose chiefs were the sovereign rulers of both land and people. This was a vast oversimplification. The "ruling" houses (*dawlas*) were in some cases not even agnatically related to their tribal "subjects." (The Quᶜaiti sultans, for example, were descended from Yafiᶜi invaders of Hadramawt.) Instead, they were a distinct social class that had arisen in response to specific needs of the society. The unlettered tribesmen, with their purely local preoccupations, were in no position to make sound judgments for themselves on matters involving the outside world and were content to let those with broader knowledge and experience speak for them when transactions with foreigners could not be avoided. The function became institutionalized in certain families, from which the ruler – whether sultan, amir, or shaikh – was elected by a council of tribal and religious notables.

In addition to specialized knowledge, it was necessary for the *dawlas* to dispose of some source of revenue in order to attain and preserve a position of leadership. The most common source was ownership of agricultural land, but control of ports or of caravan routes could also be lucrative. The sphere of influence of the Abdali ruling house, for example, contained relatively few fighting men, but, as the house owned substantial productive land in Wadi Tiban as well as the port of Aden, it was able in the seventeenth century to hire Yafiᶜi mercenaries to assert its independence from the Zaidi imamate. The ability of some rulers to accumulate surplus food staples to tide the tribesmen over in famine years tended to encourage tribal loyalty and to enhance the *dawlas'* effectiveness as umpires in intertribal disputes. Some were able to maintain small standing armed forces and thus to provide a modicum of security in a society where, as described by a South Yemeni officer in the Government Guard under the British regime,

If you quarrel with someone you quarrel with his family and tribe. If they are strong you will expose your own family and tribe to danger as well as yourself. If you kill or hurt one of them they will kill or hurt one of you, even if they have to wait years to do so. If you want to live others must fear your retaliation. If you have not the strength to retaliate yourself you must seek the protection of someone who can.[3]

The centrality of material resources as the necessary condition of an effective *dawla* is clearly shown in the case of the Subayhi region, where the paucity of productive land made the accumulation of wealth impossible; no semblance of central authority existed, and the area was eventually forced into the Lahej orbit.

Resting on subsidies, on ad hoc arrangements subject to revision with changing circumstances, and on shifting balances of force, relations between tribe and *dawla* were quite fragile. Some tribes, such as the Qutaybi and Dambari in the rugged Radfan mountain chain, although nominal subjects of the amir of Dali, managed permanently to resist any outside control. In fact, in the 1880s Dambari depredations against caravans from which the Hawshabi sultan collected tolls forced the sultan to open a new road to Dali and North Yemen beyond this tribe's reach and even to move his capital from Raha westward to Musaymir. The Dathina tribes wavered for at least two centuries between allegiance to the Fadli and the Upper Awlaqi sultans before submitting to a British-imposed autonomous regime during World War II. In Wadi Hadramawt there were magnates – sayyids, and men with tribal affiliations – whose wealth equaled or surpassed that of the Quᶜaiti and Kathiri sultans and whose influence over the tribes virtually nullified the authority of either *dawla* until the 1940s, when the flow of money from abroad ceased and the balance of power swung decisively to the British-backed and -subsidized sultans.

At the base of the South Yemeni social pyramid were three categories of people lacking distinguished pedigree, the ascriptive religious status of the sayyids and *mashayikh*, the property and political expertise of the ruling houses, and the privilege, reserved to the tribes, of bearing arms. Referred to as *masakin* (s. *maskin*: "poor, humble") or *duᶜafaʾ* (s. *daᶜif*: "weak"), they made no claim to noble descent, and could usually trace their ancestry back only a few generations. That they are not considered children of Qahtan raises the interesting question, as yet not agreed among scholars, whether they are the remnant of an aboriginal ancient people later overrun and subjugated by ethnic Arabs from the north.

These "weak" classes were distributed among three strata, with social position corresponding to occupation. Of clearly the highest rank were the farmers, whether landowners themselves or sharecroppers of land owned by others, termed *raᶜiya* ("subjects") or, in the former Eastern Protectorate, *hirthan* ("plowmen"). Their status was a relatively honorable one in that tilling the land was not considered demeaning to a tribesman or even to a sayyid. Unarmed, however, they were obliged to secure the protection of the ruling houses, the largest landholders, or a warlike tribe under some symbiotic arrangement.

Below the peasants were the *akhdam* (s. *khadim*: "servant"), whose occupational sphere was unskilled manual labor, skilled work such as masonry and carpentry, the production and sale of craft products such as textiles and metal goods, public entertainment in the form of music and dancing, and domestic service of some types. A *khadim* might be employed as a wage earner on a farm or on irrigation works, but was denied the privilege of owning land or, in some areas, even of entering into a sharecropping arrangement. As the need for their services in a given area fluctuated with economic conditions, the *akhdam* were more mobile laterally than most classes of the society.

At the bottom of the social scale were the *subyan* (s. *sabi*: "houseboy"), whose role was confined to personal service to others. Generally retained on a permanent basis by one or more well-to-do households, they performed the necessary but menial tasks related to birth ceremonies, circumcisions, weddings, funerals, and feasts. Well cared for and protected by their patrons, they were nevertheless looked down upon because of the nature of their work. They had no distinguished ancestry to invoke and married among themselves or, infrequently, with *akhdam*.

As will be argued later in this book, the underpinnings of this hierarchical society with its watertight compartments were eroded, quite unintentionally, under the pressure of British "advice" as well as of the revolutionary concepts permeating the Arab world of the 1950s and 1960s. The limited role of the *dawlas* was vastly expanded, to become the effective governments it was mistakenly assumed had existed from the first. Politics and religion were divorced, and the important role previously fulfilled by those with ascriptive spiritual qualities was modified and transferred elsewhere. Efforts to disarm the tribes were successful in the Eastern Protectorate and in some areas to the west. The result was that many tribesmen, deprived of the ability to protect others, were reduced to the status of *masakin*. The establishment of bureaucracies on alien, egalitarian models, and the expansion of commerce and industry, opened up many new political and social roles for which members of all South Yemeni classes competed on more or less equal terms. External enemies of the *dawlas* and their British tutors, finally, provided weapons and training to South Yemenis of classes formerly content with, or resigned to, their dependence on others for their security and newly resentful of their subordinate status. These perspectives help to explain why South Yemen's struggle for independence coincided with social revolution.

TECHNOLOGY AND CRAFTS

In a country so poorly endowed with resources it is not surprising that traditional crafts and skills related primarily to utilitarian functions. An inherited body of technology, of less sophistication and scope than that of ancient times, focused on the exploitation of the meager water supplies. Wells, often dug to a considerable depth, were carefully lined with gypsum mortar dried to rock hardness and fitted with a trip mechanism by which water raised to the surface in leather buckets by human hands or by draft animals was emptied into troughs from which livestock was watered and small fields irrigated. In the wadis, weirs were constructed at carefully selected sites that diverted a portion of the spates (sayl) into canal networks of precisely calculated gradient for eventual distribution to cultivated fields downstream.

In addition to food crops and indigo, modest quantities of cotton were grown on the Dali Plateau, in Upper Awlaqi, and a few other locations. The fiber was spun by hand, woven on simple looms, and vat-dyed with indigo. The resulting deep-blue cloth, of which the tribesman's scarf and saronglike nether garment were fashioned, was by no means color-fast. It gave the wearer's skin a distinctive hue that won from European observers the description "blue warriors" for South Yemeni fighting men. As indigo was reputed to have therapeutic properties, there was little objection to the dark smudges deposited on the whitewashed walls of reception rooms in the notables' houses. Oilseeds were crushed in rotary mills powered by camels. Sesame oil, in addition to serving as the staple edible oil, was used to dress open wounds and to inhibit rust on weapons. With these few exceptions, the processing of agricultural products was accomplished by human hands, with the simplest of implements.

Housing construction exhibited considerable variation according to climate, availability of materials, and the relative security of life. In the 1830s, the people of Aden lived in flimsy huts (kutchas) of reed matting hung on wooden trellises – a cheap mode of housing reasonably serviceable in a hot and practically rainless climate. (The first British political agent lived in such a structure throughout his fifteen-year tour in Aden.) While Aden developed into a European-style city, traditional modes of building persisted elsewhere. The kutcha remained in widespread use in the smaller ports and in hamlets and villages on the coastal plain among the unarmed masakin, who depended for their safety upon agreements with neighboring tribes. (The tribal code of honor furthermore frowned upon aggression against members of the noncombatant classes.)

Among the warrior classes, residences had to be defensible. They were commonly built on a rock foundation (the ancient art of stone dressing remained highly developed). According to the proprietor's means, stone construction might be continued to the height of one or more stories or, in the absence of easily accessible stone, walls might be built entirely of mud or of sun-baked clay brick. The ground floor was customarily reserved for sheltering domestic animals and storing household supplies: the upper levels accommodated the family and reception facilities. The roof was terraced and provided with a parapet, often with loopholes through which weapons might be fired.

The ruling families required more elaborate establishments in order to accommodate their retainers, to store the foodstuffs they accumulated for distribution in times of famine, and to provide the hospitality expected of them. Some *dawlas*, notably the Abdali sultans at Lahej, built imposing palaces further distinguished by their whitewashed outer walls and, in exceptional cases, such alien architectural features as verandas. In the main, however, comfort and aesthetic appeal were secondary considerations in South Yemeni building, and the prevailing aspect was austere and utilitarian.

In Wadi Hadramawt, where building space was strictly limited by the precipitous valley walls and the necessity of conserving cultivable land, a distinctive style of architecture was developed in the form of "skyscrapers" of a dozen or more stories often, as in the town of Shibam, abutting one another in the manner of Western row houses. Although this style of construction was quite ancient, a great many of these houses date from the period between the two world wars, when the copious flow of remittances from temporary emigrants financed a brisk housing boom.

Like masonry and hydrological engineering, the traditional crafts of carpentry and metalworking also served the basic necessities and were practiced with the simplest of tools. Armorers produced heads for the spears and lances that were in use beyond the turn of the twentieth century, beating out the points of soft iron on the anvil. Production of blades for the curved daggers that were an indispensable article of dress for the warrior classes, together with the swords worn by the ruling classes on ceremonial occasions, continued until quite recent days. Smiths turned out knives, pots, and other household utensils and also the various hardware needed for house construction and boat-building. Little carpentry was involved in construction, aside from such fittings as doors, shutters, and window frames. (The typical upper floor consisted of matting laid over mangrove poles imported from East Africa and surfaced with a mud mortar.) Although the ancient Arab art of shipbuilding had declined in South Yemen and migrated to Oman and the Persian Gulf by the nineteenth century, some seagoing vessels were built on the Mahra coast as late as the 1930s. These were of the *badani* type, distinguished by their straight lines (lacking the curved stem commonly associated with Arab dhows), upright masts, and a rudder attached to a high sternpost and manipulated by a complex mechanism of ropes and beams. These craft, built entirely "by eye" without written plans, were nevertheless quite seaworthy. Those intended for short coastal trading voyages had a single

mast with lateen rigging, but occasional two-masted *badanis* were produced that were capable of making the longer runs to India and the East
African coast. Fishing craft, highly maneuverable and capable of
withstanding the strain of the often choppy coastal waters, were built by
the same primitive but effective methods until the independent South
Yemeni government undertook the modernization of the country's
fishing industry.

THE ARTS

Given the prevailing poverty and the austere norms set by the
Islamic religion, it is hardly surprising that the fine arts in South Yemen
achieved only a modest level of development, generally oriented toward
the utilitarian and emphasizing the use of the Arabic language.

As there was no South Yemeni press outside Aden, such recorded
literature as was produced remained mostly in manuscript. Literacy was
a virtual monopoly of the sayyids save for education in the rudiments of
the faith, itself conducted by the religious elite. The sayyids took pains to
record their family trees and to have them confirmed by some such outside authority as the Zaidi imam. To reinforce their claim to high social
status, the sayyids, notably those of Hadramawt, wrote chronicles of
local events in which the role of their class was hardly minimized, as
well as hagiographic biographies of prominent sayyids. Similar lives
were written by *mashayikh* as memorials to their ancestors' piety and
learning, as well as to suggest their own title to an inherited *baraka*.
Literary pursuits were not generally regarded as befitting a military or
political leader, and the history of the ruling dynasty of Lahej written by
one of its members and published in 1932 must be considered something
of an exception.[4] Edification, coupled with subtle political purpose, was
thus the accepted end of formal literature. The classical forms of Arabic
prosody were little used for purely aesthetic ends. Fiction, of course, did
not exist in the Western genres, although artful tellers of tales could
make a modest living entertaining the crowds on market days.

Poetry as a spoken art form, on the other hand, was a major mode
of expression. The ancient phenomenon of the tribal poet (*shahid*:
"witness") whose rhymed improvisations castigated the enemy and in-
cited his own people to valorous feats in war remained lively in South
Yemen. It was not unknown for a *shahid* to denounce a ruling sultan's
conduct to his face before his assembled court. The *shahid's* repertory
was not confined to martial subjects, but often extended to elegiac and
salacious themes reminiscent of the mainstream of Arabic poetry.

Alongside these formal compositions, which aspired to conformity
with the classical language of which the Koran was the impeccable

model, there was a large body of popular verse expressed in the colloquial dialect. Seldom written down, these poems embraced a wide variety of concerns, including folk wit and wisdom, superstitions, and contrasts (with an occasional grain of resentment) among social classes.
Regrettably, local literates looked down on this mode of expression, and
comprehensive compilations by outside scholars were impractical
because of their intermittent access and their interests in other directions. With the rapid social changes now taking place, and the deliberate
repudiation of the old ways of life, this body of popular culture of great
interest may well disappear without trace.

Closely related to folk verse was the folk song, which the South
Yemenis adapted to many situations of everyday life. Herdsmen, and
children set as guards over ripening crops, had their own songs to keep
themselves alert and warn off intruders. Camel-drivers devised sung
commands to which their animals learned to respond. Many group tasks,
such as threshing or hauling in fishnets, were performed to the accom-
paniment of distinctive songs. Lyrics were often adapted to the occasion,
and a stranger arriving unannounced at a village might be greeted by a
chorus of women and children in terms not always complimentary.

Musical instruments were quite primitive. The typical Middle
Eastern shepherd's flute was widely used. The larger tenor flute was
employed, in conjunction with large drums, on ceremonial occasions at
government centers. A less common lutelike stringed instrument, supported by flute, tambourine, and small drums, often provided the
background for dancing. Dancing was strictly segregated by sex; it was
regarded as not entirely becoming to a strict Muslim. Among the upper
classes, males danced sedately in pairs, abreast, in a backward and forward sequence of intricate, shuffling steps punctuated by full turns.
Among tribesmen the style was more vigorous and expressive of warlike
valor. Dancing was a frequent recreation at overnight caravan halts, at
marriage or circumcision celebrations, or on other festive occasions.
Women's dances were influenced by the regional nautch, or belly, dance,
performed solo. Professional dancing was the province of a special en-
dogamous group of *akhdam*, for whom the men provided the musical ac-
companiment. The dancers were conspicuous for their unusually forward manner toward men; and although their morals were reputed to be
no better than they ought to be, their art was much appreciated.

Religious disapproval of representation of animate beings excluded
painting as a distinct artistic genre, and even the illumination of
manuscripts did not develop in South Arabia to the high standards
achieved elsewhere.

The severity of building facades was often relieved by geometric
designs, traced with gypsum, framing the windows. The massive

wooden doors were often inventively embellished with iron or brass studs. The decoration of sheaths and belts for the ubiquitous daggers became a minor art employing polished stones and intricate filigree of silver and gold. Sheaths for the rulers' ceremonial swords were similarly treated, with considerable virtuosity.

The high antiquity of many South Yemeni arts and techniques, notably jewelry, is attested to by the few archaeological investigations thus far conducted. It would appear that features of the people's daily life in the countryside remained remarkably stable over many centuries. Undoubtedly, the current reorganization of society and economy will erase many aspects of the traditional art forms and introduce new manners of expression whose nature cannot yet be foreseen.

NOTES

1. The term *mashayikh* here refers to religious scholars, not to tribal chiefs.
2. "Sharif" and "sayyid" are synonymous terms in this context.
3. Kennedy Trevaskis, *Shades of Amber: A South Arabian Episode* (London: Hutchinson, 1968), p. 58.
4. Ahmad Fadl bin Muhsin al-Abdali, *Hadiyyat al-Zaman fi Akhbar Muluk Lahij wa 'Adan* [Gift of the age: Annals of the kings of Lahej and Aden] (Cairo: Al-Matba'a al-Salafiya, 1932).

2

South Yemen Before 1839

Southwestern Arabia, or geographical "Yemen," has a documented history extending over three millennia. Relatively homogeneous ethnically and culturally, the society nevertheless has always been deeply fragmented along tribal lines apparent from the earliest records—inscriptions carved in stone in the ancient *musnad* script. After the rise of Islam, further divisive factors appeared in the form of sectarian differences. Everywhere, the people have been vitally concerned with wresting their living from the quite limited resources afforded by an ungenerous nature. At many historical junctures Yemen has played an important role in international commerce, and although there was a common interest in the health of the trade, competition for its control was lively. Only rarely has the area been united as a political unit, although there is a pervasive, if vague, popular sentiment that "Yemen" is a distinct territorial unit to which common governing institutions ought to correspond. The intrusive imperial powers that—for their own purposes—drew the line separating North and South Yemen also provided the people on their respective sides of the line with sharply different political experiences, resulting ultimately in contrasting orientations between which any early compromise is difficult to conceive.

SOUTH YEMEN IN ANTIQUITY

Late in the second millenium B.C., the Southern Arabs developed admirable techniques of utilizing the spates (*sayl*, pl., *suyul*) concentrating the runoff from the seasonal showers in the larger wadis. As the silt carried by the *sayl* provided an annual renewal of fertility, settled communities could arise of a size not previously possible. A sustained common effort was necessary to construct and maintain the engineering works that diverted the floods and channeled the water onto cultivated fields, and social and political institutions evolved capable of organizing and directing community enterprise. City-states came into being, each cemented by kinship ties and further united in worship of a deity commonly identified with the moon or some other celestial body.

15

Concurrently with the appearance of *sayl* irrigation and the related building skills, the Arabs domesticated the camel. This made possible both the occupation by nomads of expanses of desert that could not previously support human life and the carriage of merchandise over long distances through mountains and deserts impracticable for the donkeys that had theretofore served as the principal beasts of burden. South Arabian products – notably frankincense and myrrh – were in lively demand in the Egyptian and Mesopotamian societies far to the north. They formed the nucleus of a caravan trade that, as navigation in the Indian Ocean expanded, came to embrace a variety of luxury products from India, Southeast Asia, China, and eastern Africa for which the South Arabians acted as middlemen. Rivalry for control of the caravan trade became a basic feature of the relations among the five major South Arabian states – Qataban, Awsan, and Hadramawt in the territory that is now South Yemen; and Saba (Sheba) and Maʿin in present North Yemen. The general course of the region's ancient history is known from local inscriptions and from classical texts in Greek and Latin; systematic excavation has as yet been conducted at only a few archaeological sites.

The state that grew up in Wadi Hadramawt and its tributaries possessed the special advantage of a substantial natural wealth in the myrrh shrub and also a modest supply of the frankincense tree; it was moreover in a position to establish a monopoly of the far richer production of the latter aromatic in the region to the northeast, the present Omani province of Dhofar. Much of the incense was carried in small boats to Qana, a Hadrami port near the present Bir Ali, and thence by camel caravan inland past the wadi to a depot at Shabwa, on the edge of the Ramlat Sabatein, a nearly waterless expanse of sandy desert. Despite its ill-favored situation Shabwa grew into a relatively important center, both because of its nearby salt mines and because a choice of caravan routes led thence toward Nejran, an unavoidable node in the road north to the great markets. It was (and is) theoretically possible to use a narrow gap in the Ramlat Sabatein and travel direct to Nejran between that desert and the Empty Quarter. This route, however, was traversable only by lightly laden camels and was thus uneconomical; it was apparently little used in antiquity. Other trails led westward to the main north-south road that lay between the desert and the eastern slopes of the mountains. These passed, however, through the territory of other states anxious not only to maximize their profit from the transit trade but if possible to gain control of the source of its aromatics component. Much of Yemen's ancient history can be interpreted in terms of commercial rivalry among the area's major political entities and occasionally successful attempts to bring them all under a single central authority.

Some 100 kilometers (60 miles) west of Shabwa is the Wadi

Bayhan, the longest of the valleys draining the Yemeni highlands northeastward into the Empty Quarter. The Kingdom of Qataban was
centered there and in the adjacent Wadi Harib, where its capital, Timnaᶜ,
was situated. The Qatabanians developed *sayl* irrigation to its highest
point in South Arabia. In modern times, about the same area is under
some form of cultivation as in antiquity (approximately 4,000 hectares,
or 10,000 acres), but with far less efficient techniques, so that the region
can now support only a relatively sparse population. Silt deposited by
the *sayl* waters accumulated on the ancient fields at a rate of one meter
every century and a half. Investigation of the area cultivated in antiquity – now a desolation of eroded gullies, buttes, and sand blown in from
the Empty Quarter – indicates that the silt built up to the amazing depth
of 15 to 18 meters (49 to 59 feet) over the twelve centuries between the
system's establishment and its abandonment about the second century
A.D.[1] The most practicable trails from Hadramawt to the northern
markets traversed the territory of Qataban, which sought to take full advantage of its strategic position on the caravan route.

South and west of Qataban lay the state of Awsan, distinguished
from its neighbors by a firmer orientation toward the sea and by a
feebler cohesiveness resulting from a more diverse population. Its territory included the highland areas in present Upper Awlaqi and extended to Aden (called Eudaemon Arabia by classical writers). With its
unique natural conformation, Aden became the principal port of
discharge for the luxury merchandise – textiles, gems, spices, and the
like – from India and East Asia for local consumption or onward carriage
by land to the north, as well as exotic products from eastern Africa such
as ivory, ostrich feathers, and slaves. The Awsanians themselves were
mariners and entrepreneurs. They planted colonies in the Horn of Africa
that laid the cultural bases of the ancient Ethiopian state of Aksum. By
the time Greek writers began to acquire knowledge of the Indian Ocean,
the entire African littoral was known to them as the Awsanian Coast.

So long as the camel caravan remained the principal means of
transport from South Arabia to the Mediterranean, the South Yemeni
states were commercially hostage to Maᶜin and Saba, through whose territory their trade had to pass. Throughout its history, Maᶜin's charac-
teristic preoccupation was the development and protection of the trade
routes. Saba, on the other hand, emerged as a vigorous expansionist
state. According to some accounts, toward the end of the fifth century
B.C. Awsan had encroached upon the territory of both Qataban and
Hadramawt. These two states allied themselves with Karib-il Watar,
monarch of Saba, to attack Awsan. The operation was successful, but
Saba then proceeded to establish hegemony over her former allies as
well as her neighbor Maᶜin, and for a century or so all the major Yemeni

states were united under a single regime. The reconnaissance mission sent by Alexander the Great to South Arabia in 323 B.C. reported the entire region as the land of the Sabeans, without distinguishing its component parts. The Sabean Empire dissolved, however, over the following few generations, as the subject states reasserted their independence. Qataban developed imperial proclivities of its own, imposing its tutelage over both Hadramawt and Ma'in early in the second century B.C.

With the revival of Egypt under the Ptolemies as a maritime power in the Red Sea, the structure of the north-south trade began to change profoundly. An increasing share of the transit merchandise was carried in ships. Egyptian merchants settled in Aden, where they learned that the spices, textiles, and products other than aromatics were not, as previously assumed, indigenous to Yemen but originated far to the east. The rise of shipping obviously gravely threatened the interests of the landlocked states and intensified their rivalry. Saba's attention was attracted southward toward Aden and the ocean. Intervening, however, was the independent Himyarite tribe centered at Dhu Raidan, near the present North Yemeni town of Yarim. During the second century B.C., the Himyarites were able to manipulate the dynastic strife then troubling Saba and eventually to assume its throne for themselves under the title "Kings of Saba and Dhu Raidan." This new Sabean regime finally extinguished Awsan as a separate entity. It then attacked Qataban in alliance with Hadramawt, whose forces burnt Timna'. The allies divided the defeated territory between them, save for a small residual Qatabanian statelet in Wadi Harib. Over the following few centuries the Himyarite kings extended their suzerainty over all South Arabia, including Hadramawt. The port of Aden was closed to international traffic, and shipping from India and the East was obliged to use Muza (modern Mocha), inside the Bab al-Mandab, where it could be more easily monitored (and taxed) from the Himyarite capital at Zafar (Dhu Raidan).

This political consolidation, however, did not produce an increment of economic strength or social solidarity. Beginning in the first century A.D., maintenance of the ancient irrigation works began to decline in such areas as Wadi Bayhan, and the agricultural base of the economy gradually weakened. It has been suggested that the prestige of the various tribal gods had diminished and with it the ability of the priesthood to mobilize the people for collective effort. Meanwhile, Yemen was losing its monopoly of the transit trade. At some date before the second century the Romans, now ruling Egypt, discovered the regime of the Indian Ocean monsoon winds and became capable of sailing their ships directly to India and beyond, bypassing Muza and other Yemeni ports. A formidable local rival furthermore appeared with the rise of Aksum, across the Red Sea, which played an increasingly active role both in the incense trade, where its production competed with that of Hadramawt, and in the internal affairs of the Himyarite state. The third century witnessed a sharp contraction of economic activity in the Mediterranean basin resulting from domestic strife within the Roman Empire, the persistent encroachment of barbarians, and chronic war with Persia. As Christianity spread, moreover, the demand for frankincense, considered an adjunct of pagan rites, decreased. The total volume of trade was thus waning and with it the resources available to the Himyarite kingdom, which had never had the character of a truly unified, closely administered state. Its tribal components sought to retain control of their local affairs, and much of the kings' energies were absorbed in military operations against restive vassals.

This weakness made possible the Ethiopian conquest of Yemen in the fourth century and an occupation that lasted nearly seventy years. Defeat in war often produces revolutionary change, and in Yemen the reaction took a religious form, perhaps, one may surmise, because the Yemenis' tribal gods, one of whose ascribed functions was to ensure the security of the community, had failed them. Monotheism was already a familiar concept. As early as the first century, Jewish immigrants had arrived and had made some converts to Judaism. During the Ethiopian occupation, missions from the Christian church in Syria established sees in Zafar, Aden, and elsewhere in Yemen. Some scholars have speculated that the Himyarite prince who led the successful revolt against Aksum and who invoked a deity called Dhu Samawi ("Lord of the heavens") was in fact a Christian proselyte. However this may be, his successors embraced the Judaic faith, the propagation of which was henceforth a major aim of state policy.

More secular preoccupations were not lost sight of, including restoration of public works and efforts to revive the maritime and caravan trade. Halfway through the fifth century, the king mobilized 20,000 Himyarites and Hadramis to repair breaches in the renowned Sabean dam at Marib. The late Himyarite kings, however, are best known for their zeal against both pagans and Christians. The last Judaizing monarch, Dhu Nuwas, conducted a massacre of the Christian community at Nejran that prompted Ethiopia, urged on by Byzantium, to reoccupy Yemen in the year 525 and set up a puppet Christian regime. Abraha, the leader of the ensuing revolt, was himself a militant Christian, but he succeeded in evicting the Ethiopians and thwarting their attempts to reestablish direct rule, although he prudently acknowledged a general Ethiopian suzerainty. Some influential members of the Himyarite aristocracy, however, were not reconciled to the state religion. They appealed to Chosroes I, the Sassanian king then at war with Byzantium and engaged in repressing his own (presumably subversive) Christian subjects. In 575 Chosroes sent an army that went, perhaps, beyond the aims of the Yemeni dissidents by overthrowing Abraha and furthermore making of South Arabia a province of the expanding Persian Empire. It remained so until the appearance of Islam, when the Persian governor embraced the new faith, as the vast majority of Yemenis soon did, and the region became a part of the Arab empire centered at Medina.

SOUTH YEMEN IN THE MIDDLE AGES

In principle, conversion to the new monotheistic faith offered a synthesis that might submerge the civil strife attendant upon the rivalry between Judaism and Christianity. But Islam soon brought its own cleavages, which became intertwined with rivalries among Yemeni tribal groupings. So long, furthermore, as their kinship bonds remained the decisive orientation of the tribesmen, they never became truly reconciled to outside authority of any sort. The resulting tensions made Yemen's history under Islam a remarkably stormy and violent one.

The Prophet Muhammad divided Arabia into several provinces, appointing governors from his own entourage or local magnates where these were sufficiently learned in the tenets of the new religion. Under the Prophet's immediate successors an administrative pattern emerged in which one governor ruled Northern Yemen from headquarters in Sanaa and another the South from the town of Janad, while Hadramawt was sometimes attached to one or other of these provinces and sometimes received its own governor. As elsewhere in the Arabian Peninsula, the Yemeni people did not submit immediately and definitively to theocratic rule by outsiders, and they particularly resented assessment of the canonical tithes. The area was in outright rebellion in the last year of the Prophet's life, and Abu Bakr, the first caliph, was obliged to send armies from Medina to restore obedience.

As the most populous region of the Arabian Peninsula, Yemen provided its full share of personnel for the armies that carried Islam to central France and the gates of China, and of the Arabs who settled in the conquered territories. They were intimately involved on all sides of the controversy between Mu'awiya and Ali bin Abi Talib that resulted in permanent schism within Islam. During the Prophet's lifetime, Ali had served as missionary and judge among the Hamdan tribes of Northern Yemen, who tended to side with him, while the Himyarites to the south inclined toward his rival. Both Ali and Mu'awiya sent governors and armed forces to Yemen, where the consequent civil strife is reminiscent of the struggle eight centuries before over the Sabean throne. Following Mu'awiya's victory, Yemen was governed by the Umayyads as a single province (save for the interim A.D. 685-693, when the influence of Abdullah bin Zubayr's anticaliphate at Mecca was uppermost).

A considerable number of South Yemenis, however, refused allegiance to either Ali or Muʿawiya and became adherents of the separatist Kharijite movement. When the latter itself divided into radical and moderate branches, the less intransigent faction, the Ibadiya, commanded the greatest appeal in South Yemen. In the reign of the last Umayyad caliph, Marwan II (744-750), Hadramawt rebelled against the Umayyads under a local Ibadi leader, Abdullah bin Yahya al-Kindi (nicknamed "the One-Eyed"). His influence spread throughout Yemen, and he sent his representatives as far afield as Sanaa. His support made possible the organizing of a Kharijite army that occupied Mecca and Medina, but it failed in an attempt to seize the Umayyad capital at Damascus. An Umayyad army was sent to Hadramawt to stamp out all traces of Ibadism; the sect's influence nevertheless persisted in Hadramawt for several centuries.

The Umayyad state was at its last gasp, however, in the face of rebellion in Iraq and Syria itself. Its Abbasid successors, ruling from Baghdad, asserted their authority promptly over South Arabia with relatively minor resistance except in Hadramawt, where the surviving Ibadis regarded the new caliphate as no more legitimate than the Umayyad, and whose dissidence was repressed with great severity. Abbasid governors of Yemen were rotated too rapidly to permit much continuity in administration, and the province was too remote to allow of close supervision by the imperial court. Some urban centers gained repute as centers of learning. The Imam al-Shafei, founder of the orthodox sect that bears his name, studied with Sanaa scholars during the time of Haroun al-Rashid (786-809). No feeling, however, of a common identity arose among Yemenis as a whole. Al-Rashid's governor, Muhammad bin Khalid bin Barmak, made his headquarters at a village near Yarim, where he was conveniently placed to mediate in disputes between Northern and Southern Yemenis. Persistent revolts in the Tihama and Hadramawt necessitated the frequent dispatch of military reinforcements from Baghdad. Under the Caliph Maʾmun (813-833) disintegration of the unitary Islamic state proceeded rapidly under the blows of sectarian strife, independence movements in various territories, intradynastic rivalries, and a challenge to Abbasid legitimacy by the descendants of Ali bin Abi Talib, who claimed to inherit the spiritual insight of their ancestor the Prophet.

In 822 Maʾmun divided Yemen into two provinces – the highlands and the coastal plain – and appointed Muhammad bin Abdullah bin Ziyad governor of the Tihama, then disrupted by tribal rebellions. Amply supplied with troops, Ziyad restored order, but he then proceeded to establish his own kingdom, independent save for the mention of the Abbasid caliph's name in the Friday prayers. He built a new city, Zabid, as his capital. The Ziyadi state rapidly extended its territory to include the inland district of Janad and all of South Yemen, including Aden and its hinterland, Bayhan, and Hadramawt with its port, Shihr. Descendants of Muhammad bin Ziyad ruled the North Yemeni Tihama until early in the eleventh century, when they were succeeded by a dynasty founded by Najah, an Ethiopian slave at their court, whose rule lasted until the middle of the twelfth century. The South Yemeni territories gradually slipped from Najahi grasp into the hands of local leaders or of North Yemeni warlords.

In the tangled history of these three centuries, motives of tribal and personal ambition were intimately mingled with those of religious partisanship. Few Yemenis were learned in the finer points of Islamic theology and law. Most, at the same time, were profoundly concerned with their souls' salvation, which, in their view, depended on the rectitude of their daily conduct, and they felt the need of guidance by those enlightened in matters of the faith. They could readily be mobilized in support of a strong personality of whose spiritual authority they were convinced, particularly when his enterprises offered the additional prospect of material reward in the form of war booty. The contest between Shiᶜism and Sunni orthodoxy, deeply troubling for the Yemeni conscience, took the form of struggle for secular rule, producing a notably turbulent political environment.

The Ziyadi and Najahi sultans relied in part on their staunch symbolic loyalty to the Sunni Abbasids, and the orthodoxy of the people in the Tihama never wavered. Elsewhere, two branches of the Shia found converts. As the strength of the Abbasid regime waned, more than one clan among the Prophet's descendants instituted movements asserting their claim to legitimate authority within the Muslim community at large. Early in the tenth century began the thousand-year history of the Zaidi imams in North Yemen, when a sayyid of the Rassid family resident near Medina established himself among the warring tribes of the extreme north, around Nejran and Saᶜda, and claimed the obedience of all good Muslims. At first, the imams' political role on the Yemeni scene was an obscure one, and several hundred years passed before their influence extended to South Yemen.

In the Iraqi city of Kufa, meanwhile, members of one line of descent from Jaᶜfar al-Sadiq, the sixth Shiᶜite imam, had organized a far-flung clandestine network designed to prepare the way for the assumption of temporal power by Ubaidullah al-Mahdi, soon to become the first of the Fatimid caliphs, in some territory of the Muslim empire. Yemen was regarded as a possible venue for the venture, and recruitment there had already begun. In the 880s two missionaries were sent: a Kufan, Mansur bin Hasan, to the mountains of North Yemen; and to South Yemen, Ali bin al-Fadl, a native of Khanfar in the Abyan district east of Aden. The latter settled among the Yafiᶜ tribes in the South Yemen highlands. By a great show of piety and religious knowledge he won a substantial following among the people, who brought him their tithes in such volume that he gradually accumulated treasure and arms sufficient to embark on ambitious operations on behalf of his sponsors.

Ali's immediate neighbor was the sultan of Lahej and Aden, Muhammad bin Abi al-ᶜIlā, who also exercised a loose suzerainty over the Himyarite prince Jaᶜfar bin Ibrahim al-Manakhi, ruler of the Janad region, whose seat was at Mudhaykhira, near the present town of Udayn. Exploiting a current dispute between the sultan and his vassal, Ali bin al-Fadl allied himself with al-Manakhi to attack the sultan, whom they defeated and plundered his considerable wealth. Then, accusing his ally of unjust rule, Ali turned upon him and seized his domain. After publicly proclaiming his allegiance to the Mahdi Ubaidullah, he mounted an unsuccessful attempt against the Ziyadi state in the Tihama, then turned northward and seized Sanaa, then in the hands of the Yuᶜfirid princes. His success had gone to his head, however. He renounced his fealty to the Fatimids and ruled as an independent monarch. This brought him into inconclusive conflict with his erstwhile colleague, Mansur bin Hasan. Ali was assassinated in 915, and his state promptly disintegrated. Mansur's domain in the North also collapsed when he died in 944. Yemen relapsed into a mosaic of small entities governed by Sunni princes. The Fatimids meanwhile inaugurated their caliphate in North Africa and shortly moved their capital to Egypt. Their movement in Yemen was forced underground for a time, all public prayers invoking the name of the Abbasid caliph. Their cause was revived by Ali bin Hasan al-Sulayhi, whose reign in their name, with that of his son al-Mukarram Ahmad and daughter-in-law Arwa bint Ahmad, spanned the years 1045–1138.

Upon the extinction of the Ziyadi state, Aden severed its connection with the North Yemeni Tihama and became independent under a local dynasty founded by Ali bin Maᶜn. Ali al-Sulayhi quite possibly had the military capability of annexing South Yemen to his North Yemeni kingdom outright. His paramount ambitions, however, were directed northward to the holy cities in Hijaz, and he contented himself with imposing on the Maᶜnids his suzerainty, symbolic obedience to the Fatimids, and the payment of Aden's net revenue to Arwa bint Ahmad as a dowry upon her marriage to al-Mukarram Ahmad. Iraq and the Persian Gulf having fallen into political disarray, the axis of international trade had again shifted westward to the Red Sea. It is a noteworthy indication of South Yemen's rising prosperity even in these troubled times that

Arwa received around 100,000 dinars annually in the first years of the arrangement.

In 1066 Ali al-Sulayhi was ambushed and slain, in the Tihama en route to the pilgrimage at Mecca, by the Najah princes, whose regime Ali had temporarily suppressed. The Maʿnids in Aden took this opportunity to suspend their payments to Arwa. Nearly all the petty chiefs in North Yemen had revolted against Sulayhid rule, and it was not until 1075 that al-Mukarram Ahmad had restored his authority sufficiently to move on Aden. As his forces approached, the ruling Maʿnid, Muhammad bin Maʿn, fled to his family base at Ahwar, in Lower Awlaqi. The Sulayhid king installed as joint rulers of South Yemen two brothers who had served him as military commanders: Abbas and Masʿūd, of the Yam tribe of the Hamdan confederation in North Yemen, who inaugurated the Zurayʿid dynasty (named for Zurayʿ, Abbas's son, who succeeded the two founders). This dynasty reigned until the Ayyubid conquest in 1174. Until al-Mukarram's death, Queen Arwa's dowry was paid regularly. Later, when she became sole sovereign of a truncated and declining Sulayhid state centered at Dhu Jibla, the Zurayʿids' relative strength (notwithstanding their inveterate family quarrels) enabled them to decrease and finally to terminate their tribute. Upon Arwa's death they absorbed the remnants of the Sulayhid domain. Already, they had been appointed by the Fatimid court as its representatives in Yemen.

By the mid-twelfth century the Najah state had fallen into decline through dynastic rivalries, harem intrigues, and licentious living. As frequently happened in medieval Islam, the parlous situation encouraged the rise of a millenarian movement. Ali bin Mahdi al-Ruʿayni, a Himyarite favorite of the queen mother, proclaimed himself *mahdi* (the awaited messiah). In 1150 he mobilized tribal forces and invested Zabid. The people of the capital appealed for help to the Zaidi imam, Ahmad bin Sulaiman, who descended from the mountains and lifted the siege. When he learned of the dissolute conduct of the reigning Najah prince, however, he demanded that the prince be put to death. This done, the imam returned abruptly to the highlands, leaving Zabid at the mercy of the Mahdi. The latter soon obliterated the Najah regime and assumed rule in his own name, even terminating mention of the Abbasid caliph in the public prayers. Ali survived his seizure of Zabid by only a few months, but his two sons carried forward his ambitious plans to conquer all Yemen. The Zurayʿid kingdom was a major target of their designs. They succeeded in occupying Lahej as well as the entire province of Janad, but failed in the attempt to conquer Aden. The Zurayʿids allied themselves with their kinsmen, the Hatim Sultans of Hamdan then in power in Sanaa, and forced the Mahdists back to the North Yemeni Tihama.

YEMEN UNDER FOREIGN RULE

Saladin and his Ayyubid relatives conquered Egypt during the 1160s, evicted the Crusaders, and extinguished the schismatic Fatimid caliphate in 1171, Saladin himself becoming sultan of Egypt. These operations had been undertaken under the suzerainty of Nur al-Din al-Zinji, sultan of Syria. The Ayyubids' hold over Egypt therefore being precarious, they cast about for a territory they might possess in full independence. The fragmentation and political weakness of Yemen attracted their attention. They had already received appeals for succor from the Sulaymani sharifs, ruling in the present-day Saudi province of Asir, who were at war with the Mahdist state. An attack upon Yemen could furthermore be endowed with a high moral aura by proclaiming the objective of restoring the Tihama to symbolic loyalty to the Abbasid caliphate.

The Ayyubid army, commanded by Saladin's brother Turanshah, occupied the Tihama with ease and overran all Yemen within a year, whereupon Turanshah returned to Egypt, leaving military governors in charge of the various provinces. Left to their own devices, however, the governors began to comport themselves as independent potentates, quarreling one with another and even striking coins in their own names. The governor of Aden and Lahej invaded and annexed Hadramawt. Fearing that Yemen might slip from his family's grasp, Saladin sent a younger brother, Tughtakin, to restore Ayyubid authority. Under Sultan Tughtakin and his son and successor, Ismail, the rudiments of organized government were introduced, aimed primarily at maximizing state revenues. Although the emphasis was on exploiting agricultural production, trade was not neglected; improvements were made in the facilities and administration of the port of Aden. Although rapacious and oppressive (as it was in Egypt), Ayyubid rule in the South Yemen lowlands was efficient enough to preserve a degree of civil tranquility and prosperity. The highland tribes, having no wealth worth a tax-gathering effort, were left largely to themselves. In the North Yemen mountains the Ayyubids never fully succeeded in crushing the indigenous regimes – the Zaidi imams at Saʿda and the Hatim sultans near Sanaa.

THE RASULID ERA

In 1229 the last Ayyubid sultan in Yemen, al-Masʿud Yusif, was summoned by his father, the sultan of Egypt, to govern Syria. Upon his departure from Yemen, Masʿud entrusted the regency to his tutor, Nur al-Din Umar bin Ali al-Rasul, furthermore giving him authorization to assume sovereignty over the country in the event of Masʿud's death.

Mas^cud died, in fact, on his journey northward, and Nur al-Din became the first sultan of the Rasulid dynasty, which was to endure well over two centuries. The Ayyubids, enmeshed in their family disputes and their wars with Crusaders and Seljuq Turks, lacked the energy to reassert their control of Yemen. By subtle political maneuver, Nur al-Din gradually consolidated his independence, soon legitimized by an official charter from the Abbasid caliph.

The Rasulids were descended from the Ghassanid kings in Syria, themselves originally Sabeans from Yemen. By religion, moreover, they were impeccably orthodox Sunnis and embraced the Shafei rite preponderant in Yemen. These attributes helped to bolster the legitimacy of the Rasulids' rule in the eyes of their Yemeni subjects. After 1257, when the last Egyptian Ayyubid was murdered and the dynasty's slave-soldiers, the Mamelukes, ruled Egypt, the Rasulids had nothing further to fear from their former suzerains. The Mamelukes warred with the early Rasulid kings for control of Mecca and Medina but never posed a military threat to their base in Yemen.

A common interest in the wealth to be derived from international trade, in fact, encouraged Egyptian-Yemeni cooperation, and historical circumstances were unusually favorable. By the early thirteenth century the Mongols had thrown Central Asia into turmoil, and traffic by the land route from China and India had virtually ceased. Rich mercantile republics had arisen in Italy. Western Europe generally had recovered from the economic stagnation of early medieval times, and demand for the East's exotic products had enormously expanded. The Persian Gulf was a chaos of piracy and strife. The Red Sea was now by far the most attractive and feasible route from India and East Asia to Syria and Egypt, the supply points for the Mediterranean basin.

The Rasulids adopted Zabid as their winter capital, moving for the summer to the more equable climate at Taiz, but they occasionally visited Aden, with which they were deeply concerned as a vital revenue source. The dynasty's chronicles are replete with succession struggles, in which the preference of the commanders of its slave armies was often the deciding factor; with defensive action against their hostile neighbors—the Zaidi imams, the Sulaymani sharifs, and minor warlords; and with suppression of tribal revolts. This turbulence, however, was a surface phenomenon under which a highly sophisticated and efficient bureaucracy operated to maximize agricultural production (and reap from it the most abundant revenue possible) and to ensure the profitable conduct of the transit trade both by sea and by camel caravan, which remained an important commercial channel. A career civil service staffed with the government apparatus, trained in mosque schools with permanent *waqf* (pious endowments) donated by the sultans, their wives, and even their eunuchs. Yemen achieved a level of civilization under their regime quite comparable to that of the other major Islamic states of the period and a prosperity that it has not known since.

Administration did not reach all sectors of South Yemeni society, however. Notably pragmatic, the Rasulids concentrated their governing effort on the lowlands, where extensive agriculture was feasible; on the principal trading towns; and on the routes linking them. Tribesmen in the mountains or the semidesert areas of the coastal plain, who produced no significant economic surplus, were left largely to themselves except when they obstructed the flow of traffic and either were bribed to desist or became the object of punitive operations by the army. The failure to devise an effective policy to integrate the tribes into the society and economy had unfortunate long-term consequences. In the North Yemen Tihama some intensively cultivated areas were abandoned and the people became transhumants or pure nomads. The same process occurred in South Yemen in such areas as Abyan when the central authority of the Rasulids began its decline.

For a century and a half the dynasty kept power in its own hands, without associating local magnates in the conduct of public affairs. During the first decades of the fifteenth century this policy was relaxed. Regional leaders began to assert a voice in determining the succession and to supplant the bureaucracy at the lower administrative levels. After 1442, several Rasulids contended for the throne for a full decade. The consequent disruption provided opportunity for the Tahirids, a clan of notables already intermarried with the royal family and serving as its governors at Aden, to usurp the entire Rasulid domain.

The Tahirids were descended from the Prophet's tribe of Quraysh and had long resided at Juban, in the Radaᶜ region of North Yemen. The Yemeni chroniclers represented them as wise, pious, and humane rulers, sound administrators, and great builders of mosques and other public monuments, as well as courageous soldiers—a quality they had ample occasion to demonstrate. They inherited a kingdom considerably reduced as a result of protracted strife and also of declining wealth. Civil disorder had brought caravan traffic nearly to a standstill not only in the former Rasulid domain itself but also in North Yemen, where a period of weakness in the Zaidi imamate had allowed free rein to the ambitions of local warlords. Aden, moreover, had again lost its preponderant position in international trade. The port of Hormuz had recently been constructed and had enticed a substantial volume of the East's exports to the Persian Gulf route. The Mameluke sultans of Egypt, now in control of Hijaz, had developed the port of Jidda; they had entered into close diplomatic relations with the principal Indian princes, and much shipping was now routed direct from the subcontinent to Jidda, bypassing Aden and other Yemeni ports.

After establishing his authority in Aden, the first Tahirid sultan, al-Zafir ʿAmir bin Tahir, moved to recover the Tihama, where the Rasulids' mamelukes had rebelled and set up an autonomous entity. They were brought to heel by a tribal force from the Tahirid home base in the North Yemen highlands, and the sultan then moved against the recalcitrant Maʿaziba tribe in the Tihama. While he was thus preoccupied, the lord of the Hadrami port of Shihr took the opportunity to attack Aden by sea and occupied the town in 1457. The sultan hastened to the port with a large host. The invaders sought to withdraw, but a fortuitous storm prevented them from boarding their ships and all were taken prisoner. A few years later the sultan mounted a successful retaliatory expedition against Shihr, which he annexed, appointing his own governor there.

North Yemenis themselves, the Tahirids consistently strove to extend their territory northward. Sultan al-Zafir ʿAmir died suddenly in 1466 upon receiving news of the defeat of his army, which was besieging Sanaa. Although his successors returned to the attack upon the North Yemeni capital, the city remained beyond their reach until the reign of the last Tahirid, al-Zafir ʿAmir bin Abd al-Wahhab (1489–1517), who held it only briefly before his realm, at the peak of its prosperity and influence, was overwhelmed by foreign invaders.

THE OTTOMAN OCCUPATION

The Portuguese intrusion into the Indian Ocean, beginning in 1498, gradually revolutionized the previous patterns of East-West trade, with ultimately disastrous consequences for the interests of South Arabia, Egypt, and the Persian Gulf states that had served as its middlemen. Within a few decades the bulk of the cargo was being carried in European ships around the Cape of Good Hope. Portuguese military installations on the eastern coast of Africa, in the Strait of Hormuz, and in India inaugurated the era of European imperialism in the region, and naval action – often indistinguishable from piracy – designed to concentrate in Portuguese hands even the local maritime commerce among the countries bordering the ocean seriously damaged their prosperity.

The effects of the new situation were not immediately felt in South Yemen. The Kathiri sultans (of Dhofar origin), based at the port of Shihr, had attained a degree of prosperity sufficient to embark on the subjugation of the Wadi Hadramawt, wage war with their rivals, the rulers of Qishn and Socotra, and to cast off their allegiance to the Tahirids. Shihr, however, was virtually defenseless against naval attack, and Aden's natural defenses were a precious Tahirid advantage. In 1507 the Portuguese, under the renowned admiral Albuquerque, occupied the island of Socotra in the mistaken belief that it was the strategic key to the Red Sea. By the time they came to understand that the crucial position was Aden, the Tahirid port's defenses were strong enough to discourage a serious Portuguese attempt at its seizure. Aden became a vital haven for Arab and other regional ships fleeing Portuguese men-of-war. Its prosperity actually increased for a time, permitting the Tahirid sultans to pursue their ambitions inland.

Meanwhile, Qansuh al-Ghawri, the last Mameluke sultan of Egypt, reacted vigorously to the Portuguese penetration by sending a fleet to India in 1508. Seven years later he dispatched an army to Yemen, not only to counter the European threat but also to secure a possible refuge from the Ottoman Turks, by whom he was then sorely pressed. After improving the defenses of Jidda, the army moved to Kamaran Island, off the North Yemeni coast. When Sultan ʿAmir refused supplies to the Mameluke troops, they moved inland against his domain, in alliance with the Zaidi imam, al-Mutawakkil Sharaf al-Din. The Tahirid forces at first fought bravely, but they were rapidly demoralized by the Mamelukes' firearms, used for the first time in Yemen. The entire kingdom was soon overrun, and the sultan was put to flight and eventually slain. Aden alone put up a successful defense, remaining in the hands of a Tahirid prince. The Mameluke advance was pressed northward beyond Sanaa into the territory of the powerful Zaidi tribes, who mobilized against their erstwhile allies and forced them to withdraw from the highlands to a perimeter in the Tihama centered on Zabid. Imam Sharaf al-Din's sons, able and vigorous warriors, maintained the momentum of their campaign, which led them all the way to Aden. The latter then passed under Zaidi rule.

Meanwhile, the Ottomans under Salim I had defeated Qansuh al-Ghawri and incorporated Egypt in their growing empire. With this conquest the Turks inherited responsibility for protecting the Islamic holy cities in Hijaz and for opposing consolidation of the Portuguese position in the Indian Ocean basin. A large Turkish force was dispatched to Yemen in 1517. Those of the beleaguered Mamelukes who were not slaughtered were enlisted in the invading force, which proceeded to its prime objective, Aden. Aden was captured and made impregnable to Portuguese attack. Disarray within the Zaidi leadership enabled the Turks to extend their authority in the highlands, and Yemen became an Ottoman province ruled (or misruled) by governors appointed by the Porte. The occupation, which lasted until 1635, was stern and rapacious but efficient enough to ensure the survival of agriculture and a certain amount of commerce. Little interested in the poorer districts of either

North or South Yemen lacking significant taxable wealth, the Ottoman administration left many tribal areas to their own devices, save for disciplinary operations against interference with traffic on the roads. The Hadramawt coast was never garrisoned in strength, and the Kathiri sultans were able to pursue a devious, quasi-independent policy, playing off Turk against Portuguese.

Toward the middle of the seventeenth century, Yemen's successful liberation movement was led by a new dynasty of Zaidi imams, the Qasimis. South Yemen again was subjected to Zaidi rule, which extended momentarily to a loose suzerainty over the Omani province of Dhofar. The Qasimis, however, proved unable to digest their conquests in the South. The Yafiʿi tribes evicted their Zaidi governor in 1681 and thenceforth defended their autonomy against all comers. In 1728 Lahej, thinly populated but commanding the resource of substantial agricultural production, engaged Yafiʿi mercenaries to achieve its own independence. There being no entity, indigenous or foreign, with the vision and power to knit South Yemen into a single political unit, the region relapsed into a mosaic of autonomous, tribally based statelets, often mutually hostile, occasionally combining in temporary alliances for ad hoc, ephemeral objectives.

Trade stagnated. The revolution in patterns of maritime commerce had made South Yemen irrelevant to the rivalry among the British, French, and Dutch empires for preponderance in the Indian Ocean. South Yemenis emigrated in large numbers in search of economic opportunity to India, Indonesia, and eastern Africa; but their homeland remained relatively isolated from the mainstream of regional and world politics. When the early steam vessels began to sail from the head of the Red Sea to India, Europeans began to seek sites in the area for coaling stations, and the desert island of Perim in the Bab al-Mandab was in fact put to this use. But it was only at the end of the fourth decade of the nineteenth century that Britain, anxious over the apparent threat to the security of India presented by expansion into the Arabian Peninsula by Muhammad Ali's Egypt, whose ties with France were strong, seized Aden and thus drew South Yemen back onto the stage of international politics and commerce.

NOTES

1. See Richard LeBaron Bowen, Jr., "Irrigation in Ancient Qataban," in Richard LeBaron Bowen, Jr., and Frank P. Albright, *Archaeological Discoveries in South Arabia* (Baltimore: Johns Hopkins Press, 1958), pp. 43–88.

3

The British in South Yemen

THE OCCUPATION OF ADEN

Napoleon's Egyptian expedition of 1798 greatly alarmed the East India Company and the British government. It initiated a protracted search for a strategy by which the western approaches to Britain's possessions in India might be made secure. French encroachment on Indian Ocean and Red Sea commerce and depredations by French corsairs had already cut into the preponderant British position, and a new threat had recently arisen in the form of Arab pirate fleets based in the Persian Gulf, whose captains' zeal against infidel shipping was fired by their conversion to Wahhabi revivalism. Victory in the Napoleonic wars did not entirely remove the threat to British interests. In the 1830s France established, and rapidly expanded, a foothold in Algeria. In Egypt, meanwhile, Muhammad Ali was building a modernizing state sufficiently powerful to challenge his suzerain, the Ottoman sultan, and the military and industrial experts he relied upon for his ambitious programs were mainly French.

The authorities in India initially responded to the situation by vigorous efforts to revive British and Indian trade in the Indian Ocean basin. The Indian Navy was refurbished and converted to steam, thus enhancing its ability to protect shipping regardless of the seasonal monsoons. At the imperial level, London settled upon a strategy of propping up the Ottoman Empire as guardian of the western approaches to India. This policy was soon called into question, however, with successive defeats of the Ottomans at the hands of the Russians, the success of the Greek revolt, and finally, in 1833, the invasion of Anatolia by the rebellious Muhammad Ali. In the same year the latter, already in occupation of Hijaz and the Wahhabi heartland, Najd, advanced troops southward along the Red Sea coast into the Tihama, with an eye to monopolizing the trade in coffee, the highlands' major cash crop. Although Muhammad Ali had cooperated with British commerce, permitted the passage of British mail overland from the Mediterranean to the Red Sea, and granted coaling facilities at Suez for the steamers that carried it onward to India, it now appeared that Egypt aspired to control the entire Arabian Peninsula, the Red Sea, and the Persian Gulf and that the security and prosperity of British India were thereby endangered.

British opinion was by no means united on the outright acquisition of Aden. Much of the commercial community considered that peaceful negotiation with its owner, the Abdali sultan, for a coaling station on Aden's Back Bay, to the west of the peninsula, would answer Britain's essential needs and obviate a confrontation with Egypt. This was the view of the East India Company's Court of Directors and also of Lord Auckland, the governor general of India. The latter's restive subordinate, Sir Robert Grant, governor of Bombay, on the other hand, who enthusiastically shared the expansionist leanings of the Whig government then in power, strongly supported the assumption of British sovereignty over the Aden Peninsula. This attitude was shared by the key cabinet ministers in London: Lord Palmerston, the foreign secretary, and the president of the India Board, John Hobhouse. The "forward" view prevailed.

Divided counsel and dispersed responsibility were no fleeting phenomena in the conduct of Britain's South Yemen policy. Within two years of the British invasion of Aden in 1839, Britain's actions in the Mediterranean had removed Muhammad Ali's threat to Arabia and thus the primary object of the expedition. Meanwhile, a cabinet change in London brought less venturesome men to power and more cautious appointees to Simla and Bombay. For several years there was a real possibility that the Aden settlement might be abandoned, and it was largely by the persistent efforts of Commander S. B. Haines, architect of the Aden enterprise and political agent there until 1854, that the town remained in British hands. During these early years Aden affairs were the direct responsibility of the Bombay Presidency. The perspectives of the latter did not always coincide with those of the governor general of India who, in turn, saw Indian Ocean affairs from a different viewpoint from that of the empire's civil and military establishment in London. Well into the twentieth century these various bureaucracies debated among themselves over which should pay for the Aden fortress and conduct the town's administration and to what extent Britain should become involved in its hinterland. The perennial dispute inhibited the development of stable, long-range plans for the territory, and local officials were often left to improvise solutions to situations for which they lacked cogent instructions.

A major step toward resolving the issue was forced upon Britain during World War I when, in 1917, the government of India found itself unable to supply troops to free Lahej, occupied by Ottoman forces from bases in North Yemen, and to ensure the safety of Aden. Military responsibility for Aden was provisionally transferred to the War Office, and political relations with the protectorate to the Foreign Office. An additional decade of negotiation and maneuver was required before these changes became permanent, during which the Colonial Office entered the debate with claims to the administration of Aden. The latter, detached from Bombay and placed under the viceroy of India in 1932, was finally transferred to the Colonial Office as a crown colony in 1937. After World War II, conflicting currents of opinion in Britain aggravated the difficulty of devising common government institutions for a fragmented South Yemeni society unified only by the British presence.

THE ADEN ENCLAVE

When occupied by Britain, Aden was a village of less than two thousand permanent inhabitants, living in the ancient town of Crater and housed for the most part in huts of reed matting erected among ruins witnessing to more prosperous times past. The population grew slowly at first, but steadily. The garrison of Indian sepoys and their camp followers averaged two or three thousand in the early decades of British rule. Fifteen years were spent on rehabilitating and modernizing the peninsula's fortifications. As the settlement became secure against attack by neighboring tribesmen, the Indian and European merchants who arrived in the wake of the occupying forces began to build masonry warehouses, shops, and houses. The brisk construction activity attracted thousands of migrant laborers, mainly from North Yemen. Aden became the permanent base for the seasonal fair on the Somali coast at Berbera, which was uninhabited at other times of the year; this added another element to the increasingly cosmopolitan community. A census conducted in 1856 showed a population of some 20,000, including the military. By 1872 the total had reached only 22,722, of whom 8,241 were Arabs. The settlement was then, however, on the eve of a period of quickening growth following the opening of the Suez Canal in 1869. The dream of Aden as a commercial emporium rivaling Singapore that had motivated Haines and the Bombay strategists of 1839 was at last realized. Development kept pace with world technology. The ancient Front Bay port, suitable only for small sailing vessels, was abandoned in favor of the spacious Back Bay, to the west of the peninsula, which itself was dredged toward the end of the nineteenth century to accommodate the deep-draft steamers that gradually replaced the square-rigged sailing ships as cargo-carriers. As oil supplanted coal as fuel for ocean transport, Aden maintained its competitive position with the construction of the British Petroleum refinery, opened in 1954. Counted at 51,500 in 1931, the population swelled to 80,500 in 1946 and to 225,000 in 1963.

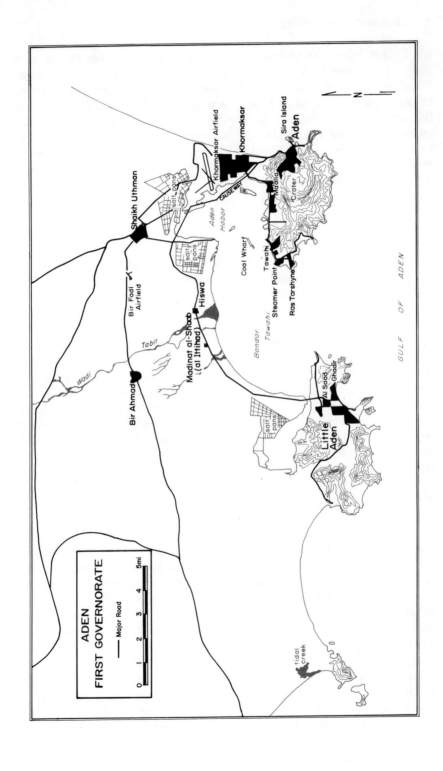

Meanwhile, the lineaments of the modern city took form. At Steamer Point a coaling station was established shortly after the occupation. After 1846, when a good road was built from Main Pass to Ras Tarshyne, officers began to build residences on the slopes overlooking the coalyards and the harbor. This was the nucleus of a borough where the colony's large commercial firms, administrative offices, and choice housing were eventually concentrated. In Crater, the rubble was leveled and an orderly grid of streets laid out; erection of reed huts was discouraged, and land was made available at attractive rents to those who built in stone.

On Back Bay north of Steamer Point, Aden merchants took the initiative in constructing warehouses and cargo-handling facilities; this area, Maʿalla, became the permanent focus of shipping operations. The British residents governing Aden, usually military men, looked with some disfavor on the growth of this community with its shifting population of migratory laborers adjacent to the imperial fortress's defenses. In 1881, the land surrounding the hamlet of Shaikh Uthman, 8 kilometers (5 miles) inland from the harbor, was purchased from the sultan of Lahej, with a view to requiring job-seekers to sojourn there while not actually at work in Aden. Shaikh Uthman indeed grew into a sizable satellite town, and its wells, on which Aden depended heavily for its water supply, were made more secure. But Maʿalla's exuberant growth remained little affected.

Previously, in 1869, alarmed by reports of French negotiations with the Aqrabi shaikh for acquisition of the promontory on the western side of Back Bay, the British themselves had purchased the land. "Little Aden" remained undeveloped until 1952, when construction began there on the oil refinery. The surrounding town was built to high standards of living and working amenity that government and private employers in the colony's older boroughs found themselves obliged to emulate. The last major step in the development of British Aden was taken early in the 1960s, when the empire's Middle East Command, forced out of Suez and encountering an inhospitable political climate in Kenya, was installed in Aden. The Khormaksar international airport on the isthmus was further improved, barracks and headquarters constructed, and a large-scale housing program instituted for military personnel, their families, and supporting staff. A causeway built across the northeast tip of Back Bay rerouted surface trafffic that formerly crossed the airport runways.

Transfer of Aden to Colonial Office jurisdiction inaugurated a process of constitutional development by which Britain hoped to satisfy the rising political expectations of the native Arab sector of the population without prejudice to the colony's status as a strategic base. An appointive Legislative Council was formed under legislation promulgated in 1944.

In 1955 four of its nonofficial members were made elective. The franchise, however, was highly restricted. In addition to a stiff means test, the vote was reserved for British subjects born in the colony or with at least two years residence there. The effect of these rules was to deny the franchise to the city's largest single community: North Yemenis, comprising about a third of the population, the backbone of the port, military, and refinery labor force, plus a scattering of political refugees. Many of these Northerners had lived in Aden for a generation or more (the days of seasonal labor migration from North Yemen were long past), but few had renounced their original citizenship. Also excluded were most natives of the protectorate states, largely temporary immigrants. On the other hand, most of the Indian and Pakistani residents, and many from British Somaliland, being British subjects or "protected persons," were qualified to vote.

Elections for the Legislative Council seats took place in an acrimonious atmosphere. There were three political parties active in Aden at the time. The constituency of the South Arabian League, headquartered in Lahej, was chiefly among protectorate Arabs, who were denied the vote. The United National Front, which drew its support mainly from North Yemeni workers and trade unionists who were also disenfranchised, boycotted the election in protest against the narrow electoral base. The field was thus left to the Aden Association, composed of members of the tiny minority of Arabs with deep roots in Aden who had become a mercantile and professional elite. The Aden Association won three of the four seats. Its platform called for progress toward Adeni self-government and continued association with the British Commonwealth. Revolutionary and nationalist winds were then approaching gale force in the Arab world, however, and these moderate attitudes had no appeal to the great majority of Aden's Arab population.

Constitutional reform in the colony continued at a cautious pace, but in directions less and less relevant to the popular sentiment against British rule. The franchise was not broadened. In preparation for elections in 1959, 21,554 persons were registered as voters (of a total population of about 180,000); of these, only 5,000 actually cast ballots. The British predicament became critical in late 1962, when the Egyptian army entered North Yemen in force in support of the republican regime that had toppled the thousand-year-old Zaidi monarchy. Egyptian encouragement and material support of South Yemeni dissidents were seconded at the global level by the UN General Assembly's special committee on decolonization. Violence and disorder in Aden intensified to the point where, in December 1963, a state of emergency was declared; thenceforth, although the forms of representative government were preserved, the enclave reverted to direct British rule. Meanwhile, the principal British political effort was directed toward devising some acceptable and workable way of incorporating Aden into the South Arabian Federation that had been formed among the Western Protectorate states. The latter's conservative outlook, it was hoped, would counterbalance Aden's radicalism and so ensure the tenure of the British base.

THE WESTERN PROTECTORATE

At the outset of the British occupation it was clear that, although Aden could be held by sheer force as a bastion of empire, its development as a regional trade center depended on the establishment of cooperative relations with a hinterland that extended beyond the unproductive areas nearby to the centers of coffee and grain production in North Yemen. The Abdali sultans, who had owned Aden, had been accustomed to pay stipends to the chiefs along the trade routes—Aqrabi, Hawshabi, Lower Awlaqi, and Amiri—in return for their protection of traffic along the trails. In negotiations with Lahej, both before and after their landing, the British accepted the principle that they would become responsible for these payments. They were thereby obliged to concern themselves with leading figures among the tribes as far north as Hajariya, in present North Yemen. Their knowledge of the tangle of intrigues and animosities that made up hinterland politics grew only slowly, in part because they were forced to rely on local intermediaries who sought to monopolize channels of information to the British and exploit them for their own advantage.

The circumstances of the British seizure of Aden had produced bitter personal hostility between Commander Haines and the Abdali sultan, Muhsin. Within months of the landing, Muhsin became convinced that Haines was involved in a conspiracy to depose him and began mobilizing forces to attack the settlement. His appeal for action against the *kafir* ("infidel") invader had broad popular appeal. It produced temporary reconciliation even between Muhsin and the Fadli sultan, whose forces had only recently raided and plundered Aden. The British fort was attacked by Arab armies three times between November 1839 and July 1840, while Indian naval ships blockaded the ports of the Fadli and Aqrabi members of the alliance. A sortie by the garrison in October 1841 against the Arab military post at Shaikh Uthman demoralized the coalition and lifted the siege of the settlement. The Aqrabi and Fadli sultans soon made their peace with Haines who, with the added inducement of military reinforcements from Bombay, signed an agreement with Sultan Muhsin in February 1843.

Although resumption of trade and the supply of produce and fodder to Aden were profitable to the tribesmen, their antiforeign sentiments

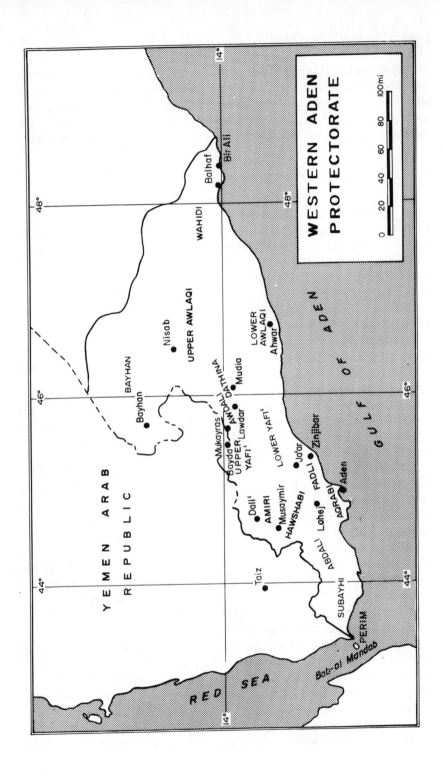

WESTERN ADEN
PROTECTORATE

100mi
0 20 40 60 80

14°

Bir Ali
Balhaf

48°

WAHIDI

UPPER AWLAQI

LOWER
AWLAQI
Ahwar

Nisab

BAYHAN

DATHINA

Mudia

Bayhan

46°

Mukayras
Bayda   AWDALI
UPPER   Lawdar
YAFI'   LOWER YAFI'

Zinjibar

Ja'ar

FADLI

Dali'   AMIRI
Musaymir
HAWSHABI

Aden
AQRABI

Lahej
ABDALI

Taiz

SUBAYHI

PERIM
Bab-al Mandab

GULF   OF   ADEN

YEMEN ARAB
REPUBLIC

RED   SEA

14°

44°

46°

48°

were kept alive by the propaganda of Sharif Hussein of Abu Arish, who had succeeded the Egyptians in occupation of the North Yemeni Tihama. Haines endeavored to form an alliance with the Zaidi imam in Sanaa against the sharif, but the project was summarily vetoed by the governor general of India. The imam had at the same time demanded that the South Yemeni chiefs acknowledge his sovereignty over them. Haines' apparent willingness to see the South Yemeni tribes deprived of their independence and subjected to Zaidi rule was resented, particularly by the Abdali. The subsequent Turkish occupation of the Tihama, however, and the collapse of orderly government in the northern highlands, brought an end to these maneuvers. Finally, the death of Sultan Muhsin in November 1847 removed the principal irritant in Aden's relations with Lahej.

The British at once embarked on a policy of alignment with his successors that endured, with occasional aberrations, throughout their presence in South Yemen. Aden's governors furnished the Abdali sultanate the means with which to induce (or force) its Aqrabi, Subayhi, and Hawshabi neighbors to respect freedom of movement along the trade routes and also to expand Abdali territory and influence at their expense. Joint Abdali-British military action in the 1860s virtually eliminated the ancient Fadli threat to Lahej. The interdependence of Aden and Lahej became a permanent feature of the area's politics and economy.

Little by little, British officials accumulated direct and independent information on the territories beyond Aden's immediate vicinity. An Arabic Department was established in the settlement's bureaucracy and a guest house set up where chiefs invited in from remote regions were entertained, "dismissed with presents," and, where it appeared advantageous, allocated stipends. Apprehensive of Arab sensibilities, however, the British long avoided any serious effort to extend their presence or to develop formal political ties with tribes far inland. The question of precisely what hinterland was essential to Aden's defense did not need to be addressed so long as chaos prevailed in the North Yemen highlands. This situation altered radically in 1872, however, when Turkish forces moved from the Tihama, occupied the interior, and advanced into South Yemen, calling upon the local rulers to swear allegiance to the Ottoman sultan, who claimed suzerainty over the entire Arabian Peninsula.

At first viewing the Turkish encroachment with equanimity, the government of India was moved to action when, in December 1872 and again the following month, the Turkish governor of Yemen, Ahmad Mukhtar, peremptorily summoned Sultan Fadl Muhsin of Lahej to submit to Ottoman authority. In a notification to the Porte in May 1873 the

British government listed nine South Yemeni tribes whose independence
it desired to see respected (Abdali, Alawi, Aqrabi, Awlaqi, Dali, Fadli,
Hawshabi, Subayhi, and Yafiᶜ). Undeterred, the Ottoman troops overran
Hawshabi, whose sultan was forced to change sides. Rival brothers of
Sultan Fadl Muhsin were subverted and joined the Turks. The latter sent
forces into Lahej, and the government of India hastily sent naval and
ground reinforcements. Britain warned the Porte that war would result if
it failed to restrain its subordinates in Yemen. The Ottoman forces in
Lahej and Hawshabi were withdrawn in December 1873. British forces
assisted Sultan Fadl in crushing his local opposition, while the Hawshabi
sultan, having lost part of his cultivated lands to the Abdali, was forced
to make his peace with the Aden authorities.

The area comprised in Britain's 1873 notification to the Porte was
not based on any objective appraisal of India's own economic and
strategic needs. It was ostensibly justified by the claim that the nine
tribes were in treaty relations with Britain and that British officials acted
as mediators in their mutual disputes. In reality, the area coincided with
the long-standing political orbit of the Abdali sultans, on whose advice
the British relied heavily, and whose agricultural lands in Wadi Tiban
gave them income sufficient to play a central political role the small
population of their territory could not otherwise have supported. This
configuration had taken shape in the eighteenth century, when Yafiᶜ
tribes had assisted the Abdali in asserting their independence from the
Zaidi imams. The British were now paying the stipends for protection of
the trade routes to certain Subayhi shaikhs, the amir of Dali, and the
Hawshabi sultan. Fadli, outside Aden's trade pattern, had been the object
of a British punitive expedition in 1866, followed by the signing of a
treaty. An antislavery treaty had been concluded with the Awlaqi, but
the principal British interest in this tribe was its ability to deter Fadli
forays against Lahej. Aden's immediate neighbor, Aqrabi, was of obvious
British concern, but contact had been tenuous at best with Alawi and
Yafiᶜ.

Once the sphere of British interest had been formally declared,
however, it took on a certain vitality of its own, forcing the local
authorities in Aden to concern themselves more directly with the states
involved and to react to any encroachment upon them. The Porte, notwithstanding the 1873 withdrawal of its forces from South Yemen, did
not renounce its claim to sovereignty over the area, and its administrators pursued their intrigues with the rulers to the south. The latter
were furthermore drawn into North Yemeni affairs by the protracted
rebellion against Ottoman rule by the Zaidi imams, who cultivated the
South Yemeni rulers as a channel for arms imports, the Zaidi outlets to
the sea being under Turkish occupation.

Meanwhile the scramble by European powers for shares in African territory had brought France and Germany to that continent's eastern coast, with the prospect of further advances eastward along the Arabian Sea. In 1886 the authorities in India recommended to London that such moves be preempted by the conclusion of treaties of protection with the local rulers along the entire southern coast of the Arabian Peninsula as well as with the landlocked entities among the nine tribes identified in 1873 as important to Aden's commerce and security: Hawshabi, Alawi, and Dali (although the latter was provisionally considered expendable as a bargaining counter with the Turks). The program was instituted at once with the negotiation of a treaty with the Mahra sultan, whose island of Socotra was the most exposed point in the presumably threatened area. A flurry of diplomatic activity during the several ensuing years produced a comprehensive network of treaties with the coastal rulers.

The border with the Ottoman province of Yemen meanwhile remained undefined. Frontier incidents frequently occurred, with disturbing repercussions on British-Ottoman relations. In 1901 it was agreed that a joint boundary commission would be formed to lay out on the ground the respective limits of British and Turkish authority. The commission's work went forward fitfully, in the shadow of shows of military force on both sides. A line was eventually agreed upon among the commissioners in May 1904, extending from the Bab al-Mandab inland to a point south of the North Yemeni town of Harib. The Porte attempted to reopen several aspects of the settlement, but after a British show of naval force in the Red Sea threatening to sever the supply line of the Turkish forces in Yemen the Ottoman governor in Sanaa was ordered to sign a procès-verbal giving satisfaction to the British on most disputed points. The Ottoman sultan, however, refused to ratify the document, and the demarcation thus remained in limbo until it was included in the general agreement of 1913 between the two powers.

The test of strength accompanying the boundary commission's labors resulted in Turkish withdrawal from lands claimed by the Dali amir and thus opened up to direct British contact areas to the northeast previously beyond reach: Upper Yafiꜥ, Upper Awlaqi, and Bayhan. With the inclusion of these entities in Britain's treaty structure, the Aden Protectorate received its definitive geographical configuration (although the boundary eastward from Harib, along the southern edge of the Empty Quarter, remained undemarcated and remains so today).

In terms of practical politics, however, the area was "protected" in only a limited sense. Initiatives taken during Lord Curzon's tenure as governor of India early in the twentieth century to extend the benefits of enlightened rule to the Yemeni hinterland were summarily reversed by London, and the troops that had protected the demarcation team were ordered withdrawn to Aden. Intrigue by both Turks and the Zaidi imam continued, facilitated by the general weakening of the South Yemeni social fabric produced by the massive introduction of modern rifles among the tribesmen, which intensified feuds among families, clans, and tribes and encouraged their defiance of any central authority, including that of the nominal rulers of the various states.

World War I further weakened Britain's position in the protected states. Because the Zaidi imam remained loyal to the Turks, the latter were able to advance deeply into the Aden Protectorate. Throughout the conflict, they occupied Lahej, only 33 kilometers (20 miles) from Aden, the Hawshabi sultanate, the parts of Dali, Alawi, Awdali, and other border regions. In 1918, when the Turks were expelled from Arabia, South Yemen was left face to face with the (now fully independent) Zaidi imam, Yahya, who stubbornly pressed his claim to sovereignty over all South Arabia by propaganda, force of arms, and exploitation of inter-tribal animosities that inhibited cooperation even among South Yemeni tribes opposed to Zaidi rule.

British policy still precluded the expense, and the direct intervention in local affairs, that would have been involved in stationing its own forces along the North Yemeni border. For a decade the alternative expedient was followed of providing liberal supplies of weapons and funds to those rulers who were disposed to defend themselves against Zaidi encroachment. British help made it possible for them to maintain small, but permanent, armed forces. In this way, the rulers' control over their unruly tribes was enhanced, while their dependence upon Britain was also increased.

At the end of the 1920s, however, the Royal Air Force (RAF) was given responsibility for Aden's defense, and this proved decisive in containing the Zaidi threat. To replace the British ground troops, now withdrawn, a local force—the Aden Protectorate Levies—was raised, with the mission of defending the entire protectorate from outside attack: the first successful attempt under British rule to deal with the Western Protectorate as a single political entity. RAF operations against the imam's forces and their bases north of the frontier were so effective that in 1934 the imam, then on the brink of war with Ibn Saud, his neighbor to the north, was ready to resume the negotiations for a treaty with Britain that had proceeded fitfully and fruitlessly for fifteen years. Brief as it was, the Treaty of Sanaa, signed in that year, contained ambiguities that were incessantly to plague relations between North Yemen and the United Kingdom. It nevertheless procured the provisional withdrawal of the imam's forces to the north of the British-Ottoman line; it established consultative procedures for handling border incidents that proved occasionally effective. Imam Yahya lifted an embargo on trade with Aden and the protectorate that had caused hardship in the South, while Britain assumed responsibility for security of traffic on the roads between North Yemen and the port of Aden.

The shift to air defense had already entailed a more active British posture within the protectorate. For the RAF, the earliest possible advance warning of an attack was required. Political officers therefore had to be moved out to the remote border areas to maintain an intelligence network. Landing strips and servicing facilities had to be built for the short-range aircraft of those days. When Britain incurred a treaty obligation to protect the roads, the disciplining of predatory tribesmen could no longer be simply left to the chiefs, even with their subsidized tribal guards. Impetus was thus added to the developing sentiment in the Colonial Office, and among British officials in Aden, that the people of the protectorate should no longer be left to fend for themselves, but should be given the advantages of orderly, efficient government along the lines of British democracy.

In 1929 the Aden officials had convened a conference of the protectorate rulers and principal chiefs for the purpose of persuading them to settle their mutual quarrels and form a common front against the threat from the north. The animosities proved too ingrained to be subordinated even to a vital common interest. British political officers therefore took the problem in hand. Their attempts to mitigate violence, conciliate rivals, and terminate feuds achieved only meager success. But their assumption of the mediating function, formerly an acknowledged monopoly of the sayyids, involved them in the entire range of intertribal affairs and was thus an innovation of considerable political and social significance.

Other important changes were in progress. Small schools to which Arab pupils were admitted had been opened in Aden well before the turn of the century by British philanthropists. As the colony's government expanded, the regime entered the education field to produce trained personnel for the lower levels of the bureaucracy. The development of British-run schools had far-reaching consequences. The teaching function was transferred from the hands of Islamic scholars to the British and their protégés—another breach in the traditional social structure—and in addition to skills useful to the administrative establishment the students acquired quite new political perspectives. In the first instance, a deliberate effort was made to recruit as students the sons of chiefs and other elites in the protectorate. When, later on, the net was spread wide enough to bring in some children of the disadvantaged classes, their more privileged predecessors were already several rungs up the promotion ladder in government and other large employing organizations, a circumstance that contributed to development of class consciousness. Within the very modest means available from London, the colonial regime embarked on modernizing and development projects in agriculture and communications in the protected states whose rulers were sufficiently forward-looking to accept them.

This "forward movement" gathered momentum during World War II, when famine struck all South Arabia. British officials abandoned their customary respect for the rulers' prerogatives when confronted by the necessity of reclaiming land in order to feed the population. Abyan lands in dispute between the Fadli and Lower Yafi^c sultans were in fact placed in cultivation under the protection of British troops. Meanwhile the Colonial Office was developing a broad policy under which it was acknowledged as Britain's duty to ensure her dependent peoples the benefits of modern society, including not only enhanced material welfare but also efficient, responsive government. In the Aden Protectorate, the British presence rested on treaties of limited scope with numerous presumably sovereign, independent chiefs. There could thus, regrettably, be no question of direct administration by British district commissioners. The solution hit upon was the negotiation of a new sort of treaty by which the rulers of the principal states were persuaded to accept British advice in the conduct of their governments. Starting with Bayhan in 1941, such agreements were concluded with Fadli, Dali, and Lower Awlaqi (1944), Lower Yafi^c (1946), and Lahej and Awdali (1952). Under British guidance, governing councils came into being; small bureaucracies, budgets, neat accounting, and modest economic development programs were introduced and often underwritten by British subsidies. Although Britain's role in these changes was discreet, its "advice" was decisive, to the point where, by 1952, rulers in Dali, Lower Yafi^c, Fadli, and Lahej had been deposed through British intervention and replaced by more pliant members of the respective *dawlas*.

These Western institutions failed to take root effectively in South Yemeni soil. By great numbers of people they were resented simply because they were foreign. The population of the protectorate, furthermore, was being introduced via the transistor radio to the heady rhetoric of Arab nationalism and anticolonialism. By the mid-1950s, the British position in South Yemen, as well as the rulers who were portrayed as the imperialists' tools, was under concerted attack from Cairo and other revolutionary Arab nationalist centers. The Zaidi imam, moreover, bitterly opposed political development in the protectorate, which he represented as a violation of the 1934 treaty, and actively encouraged opposition to British influence by distributing arms and money to South Yemeni tribesmen and by providing them sanctuary. The intrusive concepts of proper government altered the structure of relations between the sultans and the tribes they were assumed to rule. Funds, weapons, and ammunition formerly channeled to the tribes through the rulers were now reserved to the states' standing armed forces or to government enterprises from which the tribesmen derived no immediate or obvious benefit.

A distinguished colonial servant intimately involved with the reform experiment recalled that in 1956 Bayhan and Awdali were the only Western Protectorate states where British officials could travel without a large armed escort. He commented in retrospect:

> I realized that these . . . were the only two states subject to Yemeni subversion which had successfully resisted and overcome it and, moreover, had done so with little help from ourselves. Why, I wondered, were they so much more robust and, comparatively, so immune from tribal discontent?
>
> I would have wished it was because their governments were no longer chiefly or oligarchic and had been converted by reform into models of what we would have liked them to be. But the converse was true. Of all the state governments, we had interfered with them least. Because they had been the earliest victims of Yemeni subversion, and because they could not be expected to fight rebels, beat off frontier raids and introduce reforms simultaneously, we had been more tolerant in their case of much that we had refused to tolerate elsewhere. As a consequence, by our criteria, their quality was inferior to most other state governments, but when put to the test of feasibility they had proved themselves far stronger than them all.[1]

Dissatisfaction with the British and the rulers rapidly reached the stage at which armed rebellion pervaded most parts of the protectorate. In 1955, after mass defections rendered the Protectorate Levies an untrustworthy peacekeeping force, the "forward" policy was abruptly abandoned. Further political development, it was concluded, should take place on Arab, not British, initiative. Such an initiative did in fact materialize within a few years and led to the formation of the South Arabian Federation discussed below.

THE EASTERN PROTECTORATE

When the British established themselves in South Yemen, the long stretch of Arabian coast beyond Aden's trade orbit eastward to the sultanate of Muscat and Oman appeared to require no attention beyond ensuring that no outside power gained a foothold there. There were no natural harbors, and the few ports, notably Mukalla and Shihr, were unprotected from wind and wave. Their main purpose, aside from serving as depots for the trade in African slaves (ended in 1880 under British pressure), was to facilitate the inward and outward movement of the

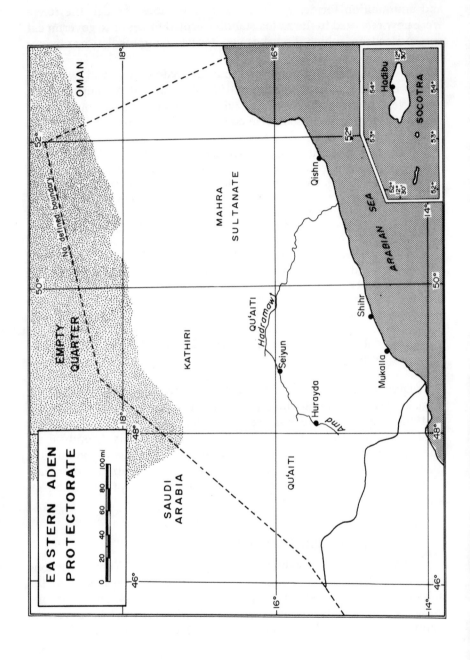

EASTERN ADEN
PROTECTORATE

0 20 40 60 80 100mi

SAUDI
ARABIA

EMPTY
QUARTER

OMAN

No defined boundary

KATHIRI

MAHRA

SULTANATE

QU'AITI

QU'AITI

Hadramawt

Seiyun

Hurayda

Amd

Shihr

Mukalla

Qishn

ARABIAN

SEA

SOCOTRA

Hadibu

46°
48°
50°
52°

18°

16°

14°

16°

14°

52° 53° 54°
12°
30°

Wadi Hadramawt's chief export: members of its educated elites who, following a centuries-old custom, went abroad to make their fortunes. In their exile, Hadrami communities in East Africa, Hijaz, and the East Indies provided religious leadership and were prominent in commerce. In the princely states of India, particularly Hyderabad, they also served as mercenaries, attaining positions of considerable influence as well as substantial wealth and property, which they employed to further their political ambitions in their homeland.

Beginning in the 1840s, a protracted contest developed between two factions aspiring to control of the entire Hadramawt and its maritime outlets, the territory then being devoid of any central authority. On one side was Umar bin Awad al-Qu'aiti, leader of a clan of Yafi' origin whose ancestors had entered the Wadi as mercenaries and settled there permanently. He was employed by the nizam (sovereign) of Hyderabad as *jemadar* (chief of security forces). He succeeded in recruiting to his cause the many Yafi' immigrants dispersed throughout the Hadramawt. His rival, Ghalib bin Muhsin al-Kathiri, who had also enriched himself in the service of the nizam, sought to unite the indigenous tribes, the sayyids, and the supporters of the decayed Kathiri sultanate against the Yafi' "invaders."

In 1867 Umar al-Qu'aiti personally led an expedition from India that attacked and seized the port of Shihr. At the request of the Hyderabad prime minister, government of India officials lent support to the operation, including the issue of weapons from the Aden arsenal. A large group of Hadrami notables, chiefly sayyids, who were unwilling to deal with a non-Muslim power but were in close contact with Ottoman officialdom, appealed to the Turks to impose a truce and put an end to the Qu'aiti-Kathiri war. With alacrity, the Porte appointed an anti-British Hadrami sayyid as its own governor of the territory. The conflict being thus internationalized, Britain raised the matter at Istanbul, where it was agreed that neither power should interfere in Hadrami affairs.

Nonintervention, however, raised serious problems for the British. In practice, obstructing the flow of Qu'aiti arms and money from India to the Hadramawt was tantamount to intervention on behalf of the Kathiri, while permitting it was effective support for the Qu'aiti. The situation became still more perplexing in 1873, when Qu'aiti control of the coast was challenged by the family of Abdullah bin Ali al-Awlaqi, the *jemadar's* principal Arab rival in the nizam's employ, who had purchased land at Ghayl Ba Wazir with the object of founding an Awlaqi state there. The Awlaqi gained control of Mukalla, and the strife became a naval war, with blockade, counter-blockade, and interference with shipping. As the two Arab factions in Hyderabad were at swords' points, the situation furthermore raised the possibility of civil disturbance and outside involvement in India's internal affairs.

After much floundering and indecision the government of India intervened decisively, imposing a settlement ensuring Quᶜaiti control of the entire Hadramawt coast. Britain's maritime concerns were alleviated by a treaty signed in 1882 with the Quᶜaiti sultan, who undertook to follow British advice in dealing with foreign powers. A further agreement in 1888 established a formal protectorate. The Quᶜaiti rulers preserved their links with India, where they had large estates, and spent as much of their time in Hyderabad as in Arabia. Hadramawt was remote from Aden, whose British officials were moreover little concerned with events inland. British-Quᶜaiti relations were therefore conducted, in a cordial atmosphere, in India for several decades. During World War I, Britain had no reason to fear for the security of the Hadramawt coast.

The Quᶜaiti were long unsuccessful in extending their rule to the Wadi Hadramawt, although they managed to control the tributary wadis, Duᶜan and Amd. Eastward from Shibam, the authority of the Kathiri sultan was nominally recognized. As in the Western Protectorate, however, the introduction of modern rifles had produced social disintegration. Authority was localized and feeble. Early in the twentieth century, the social fabric was further rent by dispute over the privileged status of the sayyids. Their claim that, under Islamic law, it was not permissible for one of them to marry outside the Prophet Muhammad's clan came under violent challenge by Hadramis of tribal origin who, like the sayyids themselves, had acquired wealth overseas and aspired to political leadership. In 1915, the Irshad Society was formed to contest the sayyids' privileged position and to reduce their influence. The struggle was waged not only in Hadramawt itself but also in Indonesia and wherever there were Hadrami communities or others interested in the area's affairs. Through World War I, the Quᶜaiti sultan tended to align himself with the sayyids, one of whom served as his chief minister and some of whom shared his desire for progress and effective government. The sayyids' cooperation made possible negotiation of a treaty in 1918 by which a loose Quᶜaiti suzerainty was established over the Kathiri state, under overall British protection.

The transition to RAF responsibility for Aden's defense, together with the receptive attitude of the Quᶜaiti ruler, made possible the extension of British presence into the eastern states. Airstrips were built from which air sorties could be made to discipline fractious tribes. Contact was made with the nomads north of Wadi Hadramawt, and a mobile armed force, the Hadrami Bedouin Legion, was recruited to maintain order in that area and reduce intertribal feuds. The first advisory treaty in the entire Aden Protectorate was signed with the Quᶜaiti sultan, Salih, in 1937. A British resident adviser was assigned, under whose supervision the traditional slave guards and Yafi^c mercenaries were replaced by an efficient regular army, the state's finances systematized, the schools modernized, and agricultural programs undertaken. A state council, on which the adviser and other British officials served, was formed to advise the ruler and maintain the pace of reform during his absences in Hyderabad.

Meanwhile, Harold Ingrams, the resident adviser in Mukalla, endeavored to bring order out of the chaos of feuds and rivalries in Wadi Hadramawt and the surrounding areas. The task was a monumental one. The Kathiri sultan, whose seat was Saywun, had no seaport and little productive land. Having only meager revenues, he was dependent on the financial support of wealthier men, notably Bubakr bin Shaikh al-Kaff, a prominent member of the sayyid party. In Tarim, a branch of the ruling family conducted affairs in collaboration with the local sayyids, acknowledging no obedience to the sultan. To the west, Ubaid bin Salih bin Abdat controlled a number of fortresses and ruled independently. He was a bitter enemy of al-Kaff, with whom he vied for influence among the surrounding tribes, themselves divided by feuds and disputes of long standing. In February 1937 members of a tribe residing between Tarim and the port of Shihr fired on a British army engineer as he was inspecting a road being built by Sayyid Bubakr between those two towns. Ingrams required them to submit to the Kathiri sultan and pay him their fine. Building on this incident, he rapidly negotiated more than a thousand three-year intertribal truces under the nominal aegis of the Kathiri ruler, the only local personage in formal relations with Britain. For the first time in years many men could set foot outside their towering fortress-houses in the wadi without risking assassination by hostile neighbors.

The success of "Ingrams's peace" was due in part to the fact that other local magnates had already been striving to make peace among warring tribes and factions and create some form of effective central authority. Sayyid Bubakr, who seconded the British effort, had already been working along this line. Bin Abdat, however, wove his own network of truces, and by the end of the three-year term of Ingrams's agreements clashes were occurring between the respective adherents to the two alliances. Little or no progress was made in instituting orderly government. The Kathiri sultan's authority remained nominal. A joint Qu^caiti-British expedition against bin Abdat met with only limited success, and after the outbreak of World War II the British for a time lacked the means to impose discipline on a xenophobic population suspicious of their intentions. Decisive action became imperative in 1943, when famine struck South Arabia. Hadramawt, always a deficit area, suffered severely, as the Japanese occupation of Indonesia had shut off its principal source of foodstuffs and the funds with which to buy them. An emergency food distribution program undertaken by the British was obstructed by the Tarim sayyids, and with particular vigor by bin Abdat, who was finally, and decisively, overwhelmed by British forces in March 1945.

The flow of remittances from Indonesia and elsewhere on which the power of the Hadrami sayyids and magnates rested was a casualty of the global war. The resources of Britain's Aden Residency now far outweighed those of the local magnates. The Kathiri state saw the rapid growth of a modern governing apparatus, backed by a professional military force, and the institution of irrigation and other economic projects. The social structure was significantly altered. The sayyids, formerly the elite, lost their mediating function, as well as their monopoly of learning, to foreign advisers or their indigenous protégés. Impoverished, the sayyids were obliged to compete on relatively equal terms with others for positions in the bureaucracy and the new schools; their moral and political hold over the people diminished accordingly.

Less directly pressured by North Yemen, the two Hadramawt states and their less populous neighbors, the Mahra Sultanate of Qishn and Socotra and the two small Wahidi principalities, felt less need to combine for their common defense. Oil-prospecting activity at Thamoud, north of the wadi, raising hopes (never realized) of fabulous revenues, proved a divisive factor. The area was claimed by both the Qucaiti and the Kathiri rulers, each of whom sought to secure for himself the largest possible share in the future bonanza, while neither found appealing the notion (attractive to the British and to Arab nationalists in Aden) that it should be used for the general benefit of a South Yemeni state. It was only reluctantly that the Eastern Protectorate rulers were eventually wooed into the unification program the British were nurturing to the west.

THE SOUTH ARABIAN FEDERATION

From 1937, when the Colonial Office assumed responsibility for Aden Colony, constitutional change in the territory took place almost entirely on British initiative. The process proceeded in a world climate increasingly hostile to all forms of colonial control, no matter how progressive or well calculated to improve the material lot of the dependent peoples. During World War II Colonial Office officials elaborated the doctrine that Britain had the moral duty to lead her colonies toward economic progress and modernization and, very gradually, to a degree of democratic self-government within the Commonwealth. This concept, which produced the "forward movement" in South Yemen discussed above, had sufficient appeal to the British taxpayer to pry loose the funds necessary to put it in operation. The Aden Protectorate, however, was quite different from colonial territories elsewhere, where district commissioners could apply coordinated policies formulated at the center by British officials. It was a mosaic of principalities governed by amirs, sultans, and shaikhs, each jealous of his nominal sovereignty, and peopled by tribes so resistant to outside influence that even the most doctrinaire of London theoreticians could not seriously contemplate direct rule by British officials. The fragmentation was beyond question an obstacle to progress. Nevertheless, as Britain's only claim to presence in the area defensible before world opinion was her treaties with the twenty-five relatively major ruling houses (and with a number of minor chiefs obedient to none of them), it had no choice but to work through them toward progressive objectives.

British attitudes toward the rulers varied. As early as the first decade of the twentieth century some officials of the Aden and India governments looked upon them as oppressors of the poor whose backward outlook inhibited the release of the people's productive energies. This jaundiced view persisted during the interwar period, alongside a romantic conception of Arab societies and the sentiment that their values should not be sacrificed to modernization. The former attitude appeared vindicated during World War II, when various rulers and local chiefs obstructed the countrywide famine relief effort, to the intense indignation of British officials.

Subsequent attempts by colonial officers to deal with South Yemen as an economic unit had very mixed results, as was demonstrated by their experience with the Abyan Board (see Chapter 5). By the mid-1950s this quite successful agricultural development project had, through British procedures of prudent management, accumulated considerable resources in the form of price-stabilization and other funds; these were drawn upon to a limited extent to institute development projects in other parts of the protectorate. In order to build these reserves, however, the Abyan cultivators were accorded a lower return in good crop years than their counterparts elsewhere, particularly in Lahej. An ex officio member of the Abyan Board was the Lower Yafi^c sultan's $na^{\jmath}ib$ ("deputy"), Muhammad Aidrus, an unenlightened and arrogant individual whose persistent allegations that the British were stealing Abyan's profits nearly led to the mass resignation of the project's European technical staff. In the summer of 1957, on British "advice," the Lower Yafi^c council of state fired Aidrus in favor of a more flexible man. Aidrus retired to the mountains, raised a force of tribesmen, descended upon the Abyan headquarters, looted its treasury, and fled with his followers to North Yemen. Arab nationalist propagandists portrayed his exploit as a heroic struggle against imperialism.

Dissidence and armed rebellion were supported with arms and money from North Yemen and Egypt. But such external stimuli were effective chiefly because, under British guidance, the style and purpose of government in the protectorate states had altered in such a way as no longer to meet the expectations of the people. As a case in point, a minor tribal shaikh was asked by the future high commissioner in Aden, Sir Kennedy Trevaskis, why he had rebelled. He replied,

> because of oppression. . . . I visited the Sultan and he insulted my honor. In the past when I visited him he would give me a present of ten riyals or some ammunition, but on this occasion he sent me away without anything. Isn't that oppression?[2]

Trevaskis later explained:

> Tribal leaders had . . . been aggrieved because their rulers would not give them arms and ammunition. It was no fault of the rulers, who had never ceased complaining that, by denying them supplies, we had put them at an impossible disadvantage as against Al-Shami.[3] But to ourselves the notion of disbursing arms to tribes which we would have preferred to see disarmed was anathema: more particularly, in response to blackmail. But as one listened to some tribal leader screaming that he would go to Baidha if his ruler did not give him rifles one began to understand that there was more to it than blackmail alone.
>
> In the tribal world precarious balances of power had come into being as between each clan and its neighbors. Each had an interest in seeing it maintained or, if upset, tilted to its own advantage. A consequence of a clan receiving arms from Al-Shami was to upset the balance, leaving its neighbors with the alternatives of accepting the fact or seeking to restore it by obtaining more arms for themselves. That they should look to their rulers for help in circumstances such as these was reasonable by tribal standards. Refusal to give it was betrayal or, as they would quaintly put it, "oppression."[4]

In January 1954 the governor of Aden, Sir Tom Hickinbotham, laid before a meeting of the Western Protectorate rulers a federation plan by which they would turn over control, except of strictly local affairs, to a central authority headed by the governor, who would chair an executive council composed of the rulers. British officials would preside over the executive departments and sit with the rulers' nominees in a legislature, while the political agents in the various states would become executive representatives of the central government. In the eyes of their authors, these proposals did not seem to involve sweeping and immediate change. They nevertheless tore aside the fig leaf of the protectorate's "independence," which had obscured the reality of British control. The rulers rejected them indignantly. A member of the Upper Awlaqi Shaikhdom's *dawla* who had attended the conference exclaimed to Trevaskis: "'They were like surrender terms dictated to a defeated enemy! Do you think we want to become a colony of yours?"'5 Thus rebuffed, the British abandoned their plans for political development, withdrew their garrisons from remote areas, curtailed development projects, and resumed the distribution of arms through the chiefs.

The following three years saw accelerated deterioration of Britain's general position in the Middle East, including the political disaster of the Suez invasion, and a mounting surge of anticolonialism through the Third World. Public opinion in Britain itself was shifting. Among Conservatives there were still those doggedly determined to cleave to such colonial territories as remained in British hands. But many Labour leaders sympathized with the liberation movements among the dependent peoples and furthermore opposed the expense in money and lives required to maintain British authority over them. These conflicting attitudes made the formulation and conduct of stable policy a difficult matter at best and raised the likelihood that a decision once adopted might be reversed upon a change of government in London. This helps to explain the hesitancy and vacillation that marked the final years of the British presence in South Yemen.

Some decisive action was forced upon the protecting power by the comportment of the Abdali sultan, the youthful Ali bin Abd al-Karim. During the reign of his eccentric elder brother, Fadl, Ali had led an opposition movement from Aden. In 1952, when Fadl ordered three cousins executed for conspiracy and was deposed, the British authorities consented to the *dawla*'s election of Ali as his successor on condition that he sign an advisory treaty. Personable and progressive, he had been well regarded by British officials. However, he proved as determined as many of his predecessors to keep the British at arm's length and as ambitious to extend Abdali influence over the other protectorate states. He fell under the spell of Gamal Abdul Nasser when the latter emerged as the charismatic leader of the Arab masses. He encouraged the efforts of the South Arabian League (SAL), headquartered in Lahej, to win public opinion to its goals of a fully independent South Yemeni state, including Aden, and union at some future time with North Yemen – objectives entirely incompatible with established British policy. Ali's intrigues against rulers not sharing his views tended to bring them together for mutual defense and also to encourage them to look to Britain for support.

In January 1958 Egypt and Syria announced their merger as the United Arab Republic, which then federated with North Yemen as the United Arab States. Reassured that any steps toward Arab unity and federation would therefore enjoy the blessing of Arab nationalism, the rulers of Bayhan, Awdali, and Fadli informed the British agent for the Western Protectorate that they desired to form a federal union. Very soon, the Upper Awlaqi shaikhdom, Dali, and Lower Yafiᶜ indicated that they also wished to participate. (All six states had been the object of Sultan Ali's machinations.) The British took the proposal under advisement cautiously, in apprehension of the reaction in Cairo and Sanaa, which in fact proved bitterly hostile. Sultan Ali and the SAL mounted a frantic propaganda effort to block the project. In February, the British received reliable intelligence of Ali's intention to denounce his treaties with Britain and to join his sultanate with the United Arab States, along with such other South Yemeni states as were inclined to follow his lead. British troops promptly occupied Lahej, forced Ali into exile, and procured the election of a "loyal" successor.

The British government, aware that it would have to underwrite the costs of a new governing entity in South Yemen, took nearly a year to respond affirmatively to the six rulers' initiative. Only in February 1959 did the Federation of Arab Amirates of the South come into being as an autonomous territory under British protection and advice. A capital for the new entity, al-Ittihad ("union"), was built for the federation just beyond the Aden border. The various tribal guards were combined as the Federal Guards, and the Aden Protectorate Levies, expanded, became the federal army. By leaving the rulers virtually autonomous in their respective states, the federal constitution betrayed the fact that the union had been formed less for shared constructive ends among the founders than simply to pool their strength against common external enemies: North Yemen, Egypt, and revolutionary nationalism.

Executive authority was vested in a council of ministers with a rotating chairmanship. In the British view, if subordinates were named to head the federal departments while the chiefs ruled as before, the public would dismiss the federation as impotent and meaningless. After much urging, therefore, the rulers were persuaded to take charge of the portfolios themselves.[6] As most lacked modern administrative skills, the federal offices in al-Ittihad were from the outset heavily staffed by British advisers and technicians. This arrangement thus tended to intensify the rulers' identification with Britain. As they were furthermore absent from their states for extended periods, it widened the already dangerous distance between the rulers and their subjects. With a new infusion of British funds, the forward policy was resumed under the new authority. New adherents to the federation were gradually recruited, and by 1965 the union embraced nearly all South Yemen save for the Kathiri, Qu^caiti, and Upper Yafi^c states.

Formation of the federation immediately raised the question whether the Aden enclave was to be incorporated in it and, if so, on what terms. Although economically interdependent to some degree, the colony and the protectorate differed enormously in many respects. Aden already had an established, if limited, tradition of self-rule and possessed education, health, and other public services virtually absent in the hinterland. The colony's elite feared that Aden's wealth would be siphoned off for the benefit of the federated states and that their traditional role of leadership and advice to British officialdom would be sacrificed to the backward, "feudal" federation ministers. The enclave's political leaders, moreover, were beginning to look beyond the very gradual constitutional reforms in progress toward full self-government and independence on the Singapore model. In the British government's view, joining Aden to the federation was therefore the only practical way to ensure continuing control of its vital military base. A lengthy and major effort was required to induce agreement between the federal rulers and the Aden Legislative Council on the terms of a new treaty sealing the colony's entry into the union, newly entitled the South Arabian Federation. The scales were tipped by a British threat to halt further constitutional advance in Aden unless Aden agreed to enter the federation. The measure passed the Legislative Council by the margin of a single vote on September 26, 1962, and Aden's accession took formal effect in January 1963.

Although British relations with South Yemen now appeared to have been placed on a sound and orderly basis, a coalition of forces was forming that would overwhelm both the British position and the federation. On the day following the Legislative Council vote, the Zaidi imamate in North Yemen was overthrown. The insecure new republican government felt obliged to call for Egyptian military help to maintain itself, and Egyptian assistance rapidly became an occupation exploited by the Nasser regime to organize and arm opponents of the South Arabian Federation. In Britain, members of the Labour party, which had actively encouraged development of the Aden trade union movement, had been won to the views of Abdullah al-Asnaj, leader of the Aden Trades Union Congress (ATUC) and its political arm, the People's Socialist party. Then in opposition, the Labour party declared itself opposed to forcing the "progressive" state of Aden to join the reactionary, "feudal" states of the federation. The latter's future was henceforth hostage to the fortunes of the Conservative party, whose government had brought it into being.

International sentiment was meanwhile being mobilized against the federation. During the merger negotiations, opposition Adeni politicians had communicated their views to the United Nations. The latter's special committee on colonialism held hearings on South Yemen in the spring of 1963, at which the federation's representative was received with icy hostility. On the basis of the committee's flagrantly biased report, the General Assembly adopted a resolution on December 11, 1963, calling for the removal of the British military base in Aden and UN-supervised elections in the entire territory by which its people would determine their future. On the eve of the vote in New York the high commissioner in Aden, Sir Kennedy Trevaskis, narrowly escaped assassination at Khormaksar airport in a bombing incident. A state of emergency was declared throughout the federation, which remained in effect through the remainder of the British presence.

With these developments began a period of steady deterioration of such viability as the federation had possessed and of the position of its sponsors, during which the distracted search for constitutional adjustments that might make the union work were rendered irrelevant by the rise of a liberation movement determined to win unfettered independence by armed force, not by negotiation. Before the end of 1963 the federal army was sent to crush a rebellion in the Radfan district. Its effort failed, and the task had to be undertaken by British forces, at great cost in British money and prestige. The hard-pressed Conservative cabinet fell in October 1964. Its Labour successor's immediate recall of Trevaskis, the principal architect of the federation, ensured that it would not survive as then constituted.

The Labour leaders regarded the Aden base as a desirable asset, but not one to be retained at the price of using British troops to prop up an unpopular local regime. Dogmatically, and mistakenly, assuming that al-Asnaj and the ATUC represented the will of the entire South Yemeni people, they sought to convene a constitutional conference for the purpose of sharply reducing the powers of the rulers and establishing a unitary state in which al-Asnaj would presumably emerge as the leading figure. This course of action was thwarted by rising violence in Aden, together with the intransigence of the Adeni ministers, who now called for the immediate and total implementation of the 1963 UN resolution. By September 1965 the British had abandoned the search for a constitutional solution in South Yemen, dismissed the elected Aden government officials, and resumed direct rule of the enclave as a crown colony. In view of the collapse of public order inland, the British concluded that the Aden base was untenable; in February 1966 they announced their decision to withdraw their forces from the area by 1968 and terminate all British defense responsibilities there. Although British money continued to flow in support of the federal army, for the improvement of roads and other communications, and even for the construction in Aden of housing for British married military personnel, Britain had no power to influence the shape of the successor regime. The evacuation took the form of a retreat under fire, which coincided with a South Yemeni civil war the outcome of which instituted a profound alteration of the traditional patterns of society, economy, and government.

NOTES

1. Kennedy Trevaskis, *Shades of Amber: A South Arabian Episode* (London: Hutchinson, 1968), p. 83.

2. Ibid., p. 86.

3. Qadi Muhammad al-Shami, the Zaidi imam's agent for border negotiations with the British as well as for subversion of the South Yemeni tribes. His headquarters were in the North Yemeni town of Baidha (Bayda).

4. Trevaskis, *Shades of Amber*, p. 87.

5. Ibid., p. 45.

6. An exception was made in the case of Muhammad Farid, an intelligent, well-educated nephew and close adviser of the Upper Awlaqi shaikh, who was named finance minister.

Photographs

Reputed tomb (*top*) of the prophet Hūd at the eastern extremity of Wadi Hadramawt. Such domes over the graves of saintly figures are a common feature of the South Yemeni landscape. The town of Shibam, in Wadi Hadramawt. (Author's photo) (*bottom*)

The photographs, unless otherwise specified, were taken by Helen Eilts and are reproduced here with her kind permission.

Street scene (*top*) in Saywun, Wadi Hadramawt, former capital of the Kathiri state. Mosque (*bottom*) under construction in the 1950s in Tarim, renowned center of religious learning in Wadi Hadramawt.

Street scene in Tarim. (*top*) Palace of the Kathiri sultans, Saywun (present Fifth Governorate). (*bottom*) Note the odd mixture of indigenous and foreign architectural styles.

South Yemen became a member of the United Nations soon after its independence in 1967. The picture shows Foreign Minister Salem Saleh Mohammed of the People's Democratic Republic of Yemen addressing the 35th regular session of the United Nations General Assembly in September 1980. (United Nations photo by Saw Lwin)

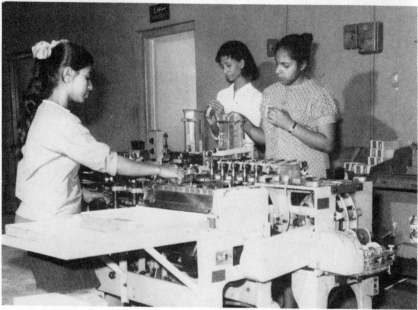

South Yemen has received assistance in planning and development from several United Nations specialized and affiliated agencies, including the World Bank and International Development Association. Here, nursing trainees (*top*) attend a class at the Institute of Health Manpower Development in Aden, which is assisted by the World Health Organization under the United Nations Development Program. (United Nations photo by Kay Muldoon) The government of the People's Democratic Republic of Yemen has taken measures to reduce the traditional inequalities between the sexes and to encourage the employment of women in occupations formerly reserved for men. (Photo by South Yemeni Ministry of Information, courtesy of the Permanent Mission of the People's Democratic Republic of Yemen at the United Nations) (*bottom*)

Fishing boat under repair at Mukalla in the 1950s. (*top left*) Although built "by eye" with rudimentary tools, these crafts were fully maneuverable in the choppy coastal waters. The nationalized fishing industry is now being provided with modern equipment. Street scene in Mukalla (*top right*), chief town and port of former Quᶜaiti state, now capital of Fifth Governorate. Palace (*bottom*) is the former seat of the Quᶜaiti sultans at Mukalla.

Recruits of the former Qu'aiti sultan's regular army in Mukalla. (*top*) Units of the South Yemeni armed forces (*bottom*) are frequently employed on civic action programs, both to alleviate the shortage of manpower and to promote solidarity among the country's people. (Photo courtesy of the Permanent Delegation of the People's Democratic Republic of Yemen at the United Nations)

Aden water tanks (*top*). As rain falls only at intervals of several years, the tanks are often empty. House at Mudia (*bottom*), capital of former Dathina state now in Third Governorate.

The Aden water tanks (*top*) were constructed at least as early as the Persian occupation in the sixth century. These reservoirs, which store rainwater falling on the mountains surrounding the old town of Crater, were restored under British rule. This structure (*bottom*) is in Bayhan (now Third Governorate) near the North Yemen border. In the past, residences of South Yemen tribesmen often had to serve also as fortresses.

Indigo-dyeing vats (*top*). Garments so processed also tinted the wearer's skin. Shaikhs (*bottom*) of the Bel Harith tribe in the former state of Bayhan, now part of the Third Governorate.

4

Independent South Yemen

In late 1967 few observers could have foreseen that an independent South Yemen would emerge as a tightly centralized state governed according to secular revolutionary principles and dedicated to the destruction of the moderate and conservative regimes in the neighboring countries. Except in the cosmopolitan city of Aden, the people were all Arabs and presumably devout Muslims. Traditional tribal identifications and resistance to any higher authority were assumed to remain potent political determinants; the South Arabian Federation, indeed, had utterly failed to nurture the sentiment of a transcending common nationhood. Such meager wealth as South Yemen possessed depended on international trade, shipping, and the world cotton market; in order to derive all possible benefit from these assets for the Yemeni people, their future government would, it seemed, have to restore cordial and cooperative relations with the former colonial power, develop them with other major trading nations, and promote the prosperity of commerce through liberal economic policies. The country had every prospect of receiving substantial aid from the oil-rich Arab states for the alleviation of its poverty, provided relations with them were conducted in a spirit of Arab brotherhood and common devotion to Islam.

In the former Quᶜaiti state, central authority collapsed well before actual independence, and youthful National Liberation Front (NLF) cadres proceeded to confiscate land and other private property, at gunpoint, and administer it in the name of the people. These activities were closely followed in Saudi Arabia. Studying the Saudi press day by day at the time, the present writer could detect the contempt in which these "foolish schoolboys" were held by the Saudis and the latter's assumption that wiser, more mature counsel would soon prevail. Some of the reasons this did not occur were examined in the preceding chapter. In order to complete the explanation it is necessary to place the course of South Yemeni events in its regional and chronological perspective.

Aside from the small, relatively uninfluential, conventional communist parties, the rise of neoleftist movements in the Arab world was a

59

phenomenon of the 1960s. Much of the development of left-wing thought took place within the Arab Nationalist Movement (ANM), founded in 1954 at the American University of Beirut by Dr. George Habash as a right-wing party. One student of the subject has traced a dialectic between, on the one hand, the frustration of Arab liberation struggles (including those of South Yemen and Algeria) and other Arab aspirations by the imperialist powers—particularly the United States, often operating through Israel and through its conservative clients among the Arab governments—and, on the other hand, the progressive radicalization of Arab thought and mass sentiment.[1] Always embracing a variety of ideologies, the ANM generally cooperated with Nasser's Arab Socialism after its doctrine was elaborated in 1961, although the ANM left wing was already becoming disaffected from the petit bourgeois stamp of the Egyptian revolution. Egypt's disastrous defeat in the June 1967 war had momentous consequences for the regional leftist movement. It irreparably discredited the "progressive" Arab regimes that had failed in "mobilizing, organizing, preparing, and leading their masses on the path of the people's protracted war of liberation against imperialism."[2] Among the results were a sharp swing toward Marxism-Leninism by substantial elements of the ANM and the fragmentation of the ANM itself, within two years, into nearly a dozen rival factions.

The principal leaders of what was to become the South Yemeni National Liberation Front constituted the local branch of the ANM, and although their opinions, like those of the parent organization, were diverse, the more extreme views tended to predominate. In 1965, after two years of bitter internal argument, a general ANM conference had adopted a program of collaboration with Nasserism, emphasizing the principle of Arab unity above all and accepting the Egyptian model of the alliance of all working forces as the correct path toward socialism. The ANM left wing rejected this posture. In its view, such an alliance necessarily included, and legitimized, the Arab bourgeoisie, which was deemed the natural ally of imperialism and neocolonialism. Socialism, furthermore, could not be built by peaceful cooperation among social classes; it required the militant leadership of the working class (to which, it may be noted, the most effective of the NLF organizers belonged). Arab unity, finally, was a meaningless slogan in the absence of true revolution in all Arab countries by which the laboring class would first have assumed power. In protest against the formal ANM policy, consequently, the South Yemeni branch suspended relations with the central party, choosing to act independently according to its own lights. As the ANM broke up, the NLF formed a close affiliation with a like-minded splinter, the People's Democratic Front for the Liberation of Palestine

(PDFLP), a relationship that still endures. PDFLP's solidarity with its South Yemeni associates was reflected in the publication of a detailed, informative account of the NLF's crucial Fourth Congress and its immediate aftermath by the head of the organization, Nayif Hawatmah.[3]

Ideological conviction thus set the leadership of the emerging South Yemeni state apart from the Arab political mainstream and placed it on the side of a radical fringe sure of its ultimate victory through inexorable historical processes. The same conviction stands as a deterrent, if not necessarily a permanent and absolute barrier, to cooperation with the West and as an encouragement to collaboration with the countries whose progress along the socialist path is more advanced. The victory of doctrinaire socialist principles came as the result of civil violence and social upheaval both before and after independence.

THE NLF'S STRUGGLE FOR POWER

The various factions that struggled against the British presence in South Yemen and the federal structure it created were at the same time bitter rivals for control of any successor regime. The South Arabian League, radical in its opposition to foreign rule, was nevertheless an elitist party, as reflected in the composition of its leadership: the aristocratic Jifri sayyids and the Lahej ruling house. Its appeal to the masses was limited to their common opposition to Britain. Supported at first by Nasser's Egypt, the league evolved toward a client relationship with Saudi Arabia. When, belatedly, its leaders realized the necessity of effective organization among the common people, the latter were already marching to other drums. The league played no significant part either in the liquidation of colonial rule or in the organization of the independent state.

In Aden, the Trades Union Congress and its political extension, the People's Socialist party (PSP) led by Abdullah al-Asnaj, had conducted the opposition to Britain and the federation during the 1950s and early 1960s. Its Arab nationalist orientation and reformist views commended it both to Egypt and to the left wing of Britain's Labour party, and it had some reason to believe that it would inherit rule of South Yemen through negotiation with a Labour government in Britain. Its organization, however, was weak outside the Aden enclave, and in the event it was outmaneuvered and defeated in armed conflict by the National Liberation Front.

Prime movers in launching the NLF were members of the Sha'bi clan, tribesmen and small landowners in Lahej, of whom Faisal Abd al-Latif al-Sha'bi was the most active organizer while his older cousin,

Qahtan, emerged as titular leader of the organization. At first associated with the South Arabian League, Qahtan strayed from it as its policies moved toward the right and as it abandoned its Egyptian allegiance. Qahtan himself became an Egyptian client, with supplies of funds and propaganda support on a generous scale, particularly after the Egyptian occupation of North Yemen in 1962. Organization of the front proceeded, along cellular lines, and by October 14, 1963, it felt itself in a position to broadcast its determination to assume sole leadership of the struggle to terminate the British occupation by armed force – an event now commemorated as South Yemen's national day. In 1965 the NLF executive council published a "national charter" expressing its intention to pursue progressive economic policies and adopt a pragmatic stance in external affairs.

This relatively moderate line, formulated by leaders who were usually absent from the country (in Taiz and Cairo) soon came under challenge from the second-level party cadres inside South Yemen, who considered thoroughgoing social and economic revolution fully as important as the antiimperialist effort. After unsuccessful efforts to persuade the executive council to convene a party congress to debate policy, they held a rump convention at Taiz in October 1965 at which the executive council (whose members refused to attend) came under heavy criticism. In January 1966 the dissidents declared the top leaders suspended from their duties, appointed a committee to investigate their actions, and organized a new "general command" among the internal party functionaries. The committee included a number of figures who were to assume prominent public positions after independence: militants Abdul Fattah Ismail, Ali Salim al-Bayd, and Ali Salih al-Ayyad; trade unionists Mahmoud Ushaysh, Ahmad al-Shaʿir, and Faisal Attas (the latter from Hadramawt); and commanders of the "liberation army" (the NLF military arm) Muhammad Ahmad al-Bishi, Ali Antar, and Salim Rubayʿ Ali.

Meanwhile, NLF recruiting operations had made deep inroads into the People's Socialist party and the Aden Trades Union Congress. The principle of armed action against foreign occupation had enormous appeal among the disadvantaged masses, and resentment was intense against all those South Yemenis who had benefited under British rule – the entire bourgeoisie, commissioned officers of the federal army and police, middle- and higher-rank civil servants, the ruling classes, and even senior trade union leaders. By the end of 1965 half of ATUC's twelve major unions had defected to the NLF, and the process continued until independence. These pressures forced the PSP leadership toward more and more extreme positions. Abdullah al-Asnaj and Abdul Qawi Makkawi (a prosperous merchant and front man for the PSP who was appointed by the British as Aden's chief minister) deliberately wrecked a conference in London held to negotiate the transfer of sovereignty over South Yemen. Toward the end of 1965 they formed the Front for the Liberation of Occupied South Yemen (FLOSY), formally espoused the principle of armed action against the colonial power, and took refuge in Egypt. There they were joined by the Fadli sultan, Ahmad bin Abdullah, who on his way to Cairo was miraculously transmuted, in the eyes of the Egyptian media, from a reactionary feudalist oppressor to a heroic freedom fighter.

Nasser's Egypt sought to induce the unification of all the anti-colonial forces in South Yemen and to keep them under its own guidance. It exerted great effort to amalgamate the FLOSY and the NLF, and in fact persuaded representatives of the two organizations to attend a meeting in Alexandria in July and August 1966, which resulted in the signing of a merger agreement. The NLF signatories, however, were members of the "suspended" executive council, and their act was promptly repudiated by the internal cadres. In the latter's view, subservience to Nasser's petit bourgeois regime was entirely inadmissible. Furthermore, given the composition of the FLOSY's top leadership – a labor bureaucrat on intimate terms with influential officials of the colonial power, a feudalist, and a wealthy comprador bourgeois – cooperation with it would defeat the revolution in South Yemen and open the door wide to neocolonialism.

By the fall of 1966, the NLF was no longer in need of material support from abroad. It had built up ample stocks of weapons and ammunition and could blackmail the Aden merchant community into providing the necessary funds. The internal leaders published a manifesto announcing their intention to break with the FLOSY and resume independent action. It immediately embarked on a dual campaign of violence against both the FLOSY and the British. The two wings of the NLF were conciliated at a conference in December 1966, and a combined "national command" was formed from members of both factions. During the following year the unified movement achieved complete success on both military fronts and assumed rule of independent South Yemen with only feeble opposition from rival aspirants to power. Thenceforth, the country's domestic politics took the form of intraparty disputes over the proper course to be followed in both internal and external policy.

As chairman of the NLF executive council,[4] Qahtan al-Sha'bi assumed office as chairman of a presidential council – in effect, chief of state – and also took the post of prime minister.[5] Most other senior government posts were occupied by party stalwarts of radical nationalist, rather than doctrinaire revolutionary, leanings.

In addition to the serious economic difficulties described in Chapter 5, and the hostility of South Yemen's neighbors to its radical complexion, the new regime lacked a basic consensus on the policies to be pursued. A major preoccupation at the outset, and one on which all were agreed, was the obliteration of all traces of colonial rule and the local power structures it had bolstered and, in part, created. The federal rulers (nearly all of whom were absent from the country upon the transfer of sovereignty) were deposed, and their land and other property were confiscated. Senior administrators and military officers were discharged or went abroad of their own volition. In repudiation of the traditional tribal structure of society and government, the former protectorate states were regrouped into six numbered "governorates." The new leadership, men of lower-middle-class origin allied with army and police officers who had received training and advancement under the British, but whose defection to the NLF was a key factor in the Federation's collapse, had no coherent economic or social programs. There was much administrative disarray and improvisation. The commercial community in Aden and the western provinces was left virtually untouched, although local NLF leaders in Hadramawt proceeded on their own toward social revolution.

The failure to abandon the rather broadly based coalition that had won independence and move toward fundamental change through class conflict was repugnant to the second-echelon party leaders, as yet imperfectly educated in Marxist thought but devoted to a vague principle of "scientific socialism." Mostly of proletarian origin themselves, they looked upon the established party leaders as counterrevolutionaries and potential (if not actual) collaborators with neocolonialism. This faction's leader, Abdul Fattah Ismail, was a native of Hajariya in North Yemen and had been among the most prominent organizers of preindependence guerrilla action in Aden. Rivalry between leaders of North Yemeni background and those native to South Yemen became a recurring phenomenon in the ruling party's internal politics.

The internecine dispute came to a head at the Fourth Congress of the NLF, held March 2–8, 1968. The leftist faction succeeded in obtaining majority support for a series of resolutions aimed at conducting a "popular democratic liberation" phase of the South Yemeni revolution. The program called for collective decision making at all levels; confiscation without compensation of land uncultivated or owned by the religious endowments, "kulaks," or "feudalists"; a thorough purge of the civil service, army, and police; nationalization of residential property in the towns; and extension of state control over all sectors of the economy. Within the General Command elected by the congress,[6] President Qahtan and his supporters strongly opposed the resolutions. The senior officers of the conventional armed forces furthermore demanded the liquidation of the NLF's irregular forces, the Liberation Army and the "peo-

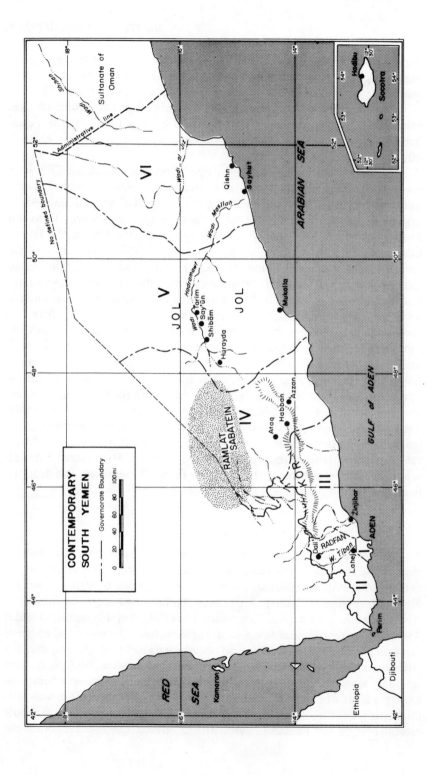

ple's guards." When the local NLF headquarters at Aden sought to organize popular demonstrations in support of the congress program on March 19, army and police forces were sent to disperse them. The next day, troops patrolled the streets in the name of public order, and the principal opposition figures were jailed, among them Abdul Fattah Ismail, then serving as minister of culture, and Ali Salim al-Bayd, minister of defense.[7]

It is unclear to what extent the operation was coordinated between the president and the security forces. In any case, Qahtan issued a statement portraying it as a well-meaning but misguided act and assured the army and police officers that their ranks would not be purged. Mass sentiment, however, was deeply aroused against obstruction of the Fourth Congress program. Clashes occurred between NLF irregulars and the armed forces. Attempts, some successful, were made to liberate the detainees from their prisons. Defections from the enlisted ranks of the army and police multiplied. Relations between Qahtan's faction and the security forces deteriorated. By June the left wing had organized its forces and was ready to move against the faction in power. Its plans were known to the army and police, whose commanders proposed to Faisal al-Sha῾bi, the prime minister, that they arrest the ringleaders. Faisal, however, contemptuous of the leftist leaders for their lack of formal education and their consistent record of failure in the traditional society and confident that the general public would reject their leadership, declined the offer. This judgment proved fatally wrong. On June 22 the leading government figures were seized and imprisoned or shot down, save for those who managed to flee the country. Henceforth, the left wing was in firm control of the National Front ("Liberation" was dropped from the party's name soon after independence).

THE CORRECTIVE MOVEMENT

In harmony with the Fourth Congress resolutions, collective leadership at the top was introduced in the form of a presidium consisting of Salim Rubay῾ Ali as chairman, with the participation of Muhammad Ali Haytham (prime minister), Ali Nasser Muhammad (defense minister), Abdul Fattah Ismail (NLF secretary general), and Muhammad Salih Awlaqi. During the next few years, the new leaders proceeded to carry through the radical economic and social measures that Qahtan and his colleagues had resisted. The government apparatus, both civil and military, was so thoroughly purged that when the process was complete hardly a trace of personnel continuity with the colonial regime was left. Casualties of the reorganization were all those trained in schools established by the British or with British advice; their successors were individuals indoctrinated by the NLF in Marxist-Leninist principles.

Sharecropper peasants were encouraged to seize possession of the land they tilled. All foreign commercial, banking, and insurance concerns were nationalized, with the temporary exception of the British Petroleum refinery. Employees of industrial establishments, down to small craft enterprises with only two or three workers, assumed control of their operations. Worker and peasant committees were formed, under the close supervision of party functionaries, to manage local affairs. A pervasive security network was organized, under the guidance of East German technicians, to maintain surveillance over the citizens and crush opposition to the sweeping changes. All possible effort was made to dissolve the traditional kinship and religious ties that had held the old society together and to reorganize the people according to economic function. The trade unions were already under party control; women and students were now mobilized in their own unions in support of the new order.

The revolution naturally encountered opposition; it took place amid violence and bloodshed. An estimated one-fourth of the population fled abroad—the foreigners whose economic opportunity had vanished, as well as native South Yemenis whose interests and status were bound up with the former socioeconomic structure. The émigrés presented some threat to the new regime by fomenting hostility toward it in the countries of refuge, notably Saudi Arabia and North Yemen, and even participated in a few minor military incursions. On the other hand, they were the social elements that might otherwise have mobilized substantial numbers of people in support of alternative ideologies; their exodus thus simplified the new regime's task of winning the people's support for its policies. Despite its preoccupation with economic problems, the leadership made a major effort to ensure that education facilities were extended to the remotest corners of the country and that people of all ages and occupations were intensively trained in "scientific socialism." An ideological school established in Aden trained hundreds of party functionaries, and many were sent to socialist countries for study, including Prime Minister Haytham, who in 1971 was relieved of his duties and sent to Moscow for a year's indoctrination.

PARTY DEVELOPMENT

Before independence, security imperatives and the desirability of a broad coalition against the colonial power had imposed a loose structure upon the NLF. Internal disputes among the leaders during the first two years of the republic prevented significant progress toward transforming the organization into an effective socialist party. The process was begun with the 1969 victory of the left wing. At its Fifth Congress, held in March 1972, the National Front dissolved the high command that had made possible Qahtan al-Sha'bi's rise to personal power and replaced it with a central committee and a political bureau. Organization at the lower levels was tightened up and responsiveness to the top command improved. The party assumed control of the radio and press, and its own weekly organ, *al-Thawri* ("the revolutionary") became the only serial publication of consequence.

Several years were required for the party to develop cogent policies out of the various currents of leftist thought among the leaders—Maoist, Guevarist, Leninist, and so on—an uncertainty that hampered effective planning and management of the nationalized economy. With the assistance of Soviet advisers, a coherent concept was formulated of the current stage of South Yemen's revolution. According to the conclusions reached, true democratic revolutionary principles had yet to reach the peasant masses in the countryside, who were the natural and necessary allies of the workers. The major objective must be to create a firm alliance between peasants and workers under the leadership of a vanguard party "which can implement the economic, social, and political program and stand firmly against colonialism and neocolonialism and eliminate the class forces linked to them."[8] The petite bourgeoisie, although itself incapable of revolutionary leadership, should be put to use "in the interests of the working class and its allies to solve the problems of the national democratic revolution and complete the process of economic, social, and political liberation."[9]

The newly devised doctrine was presented before a Unification Congress in October 1975 marking the amalgamation of the National Front with two smaller organizations. The first, the Vanguard party, was a Baathist organization independent of the ruling Baath parties of Iraq and Syria. The second, the People's Democratic Union, was a communist formation, originally under Chinese influence, which had gravitated toward the Soviet school. Both parties had been allotted ministerial portfolios in the post–Corrective Movement cabinet. The coalition was now designated the Unified Political Organization. Under the leadership of Secretary General Abdul Fattah Ismail, organizational work continued toward the specific objective of making it a centralized vanguard party on the Soviet and East European model.

Controversy over this trend within the party precipitated a serious crisis. It was bitterly opposed by Salim Rubay' Ali who, in addition to his office as chief of state, was the party's assistant secretary general and had a network of sympathizers throughout its hierarchy. Of vaguely Maoist leanings, he had firm confidence in the soundness of the people's revolutionary initiative at the local level and objected to the centralization implied by the "vanguard party" concept. Having, as president, a substantial budget beyond party control, he used it to undertake development projects managed by persons loyal primarily to himself. His appointees, however, were often inept and incompetent if not actually corrupt, and the result was much waste and lack of coordination. Although fully reliable information on the dispute is lacking,[10] it appears plausible to assume that Salim deliberately provoked an armed confrontation with his party rivals, using the presidential guard and troops from his home district, the Third Governorate, relying upon a popular uprising to crush his opponents. The latter, however, had the solid support of the militia, and the bulk of the army had already swung to their side. In fighting that began on June 26, 1978, several hundred lives were lost. Salim was captured and executed, and Abdul Fattah Ismail assumed his functions as chief of state in addition to control of the party apparatus. The party's vanguard character was asserted by its new name, the Yemeni Socialist party (YSP).

Intraparty strife did not end there. On April 21, 1980, Abdul Fattah Ismail was shorn of his offices by the YSP Presidium and given the purely honorific title of party president. Ali Nasser Muhammad, a native South Yemeni, then prime minister, took his place as chairman of the Presidium and secretary general of the party, while retaining the premiership. The dispute apparently revolved around the dissatisfaction of indigenous South Yemeni party leaders with the policy, unswervingly pursued by Abdul Fattah and his North Yemeni faction, of exclusive dependence on the Soviet bloc at the expense of cordial and profitable relations with other Arab states and their desire for diversification of the country's economic and political ties generally. The long-range implications of the change were not immediately apparent, but observers noted some relaxation of the strict surveillance over the citizenry, notably with respect to the prohibition against any unofficial contact with foreigners.

THE CONSTITUTION

South Yemen's constitution was promulgated following the Corrective Movement and later amended to take account of the June 1978 reorganization. The document reflects the country's special cultural, geographical, and social circumstances as well as its authors' determination to set South Yemen firmly on a socialist path and their assessment of the current phase of its revolution. Thus, the country is declared to be a part of a single Yemeni nation (i.e., including North Yemen) and of the broader Arab nation. Arabic is the official language and Islam the state religion, although freedom to practice other religions is assured. A broad range of civil liberties is guaranteed, and citizens are declared to possess equal rights to numerous social services, including housing, free education, health care, and social security. It is specified that the law shall "regulate family relations on the basis of equality between man and woman in rights and duties" (Article 27). This innovative transfer to the state of authority over women's status contrasts with the situation elsewhere in the Arabian Peninsula and many other Islamic countries, where jurisdiction rests with religious functionaries.

The central and preponderant role of the Yemeni Socialist party is clearly asserted in Article 2, which defines it as the "leader and guide of the society and the state. [It] shall lead the struggle of the people and their mass organizations towards the absolute victory of the Yemeni revolution's strategy and the achievement of the tasks of the national democratic revolution stage for the purpose of accomplishing the construction of socialism."

Articles 12–21 provide that the state shall own, manage, and develop all sectors of the economy according to the "substantive laws of scientific socialism," with absolute application of the principle "from each according to his ability and for each according to his work" (Article 12). By implication, the persistence of a small merchant community is contemplated, under close state supervision to protect consumer interests (Article 15).

The mass organizations—trade unions, cooperatives, committees for popular defense, organizations of youth, peasants, women, fishermen, and so on—are entrusted with the statutory role of mobilizing and instructing the people in the attitudes and skills required to achieve the constitution's stated objectives. That the regime recognizes its continuing special problems with respect to the farmers is suggested by the provision (Article 66) that the Democratic Yemen Union of Peasants is to "work for deepening the alliance between the peasants and the working class and creating brotherly relations between the cooperative peasants and the working peasants," as well as to "convince the peasants that the economy is best organized on the basis of cooperative collectivism."

The structure of executive authority closely follows the Soviet model. Ultimate authority and sovereignty are vested in a People's Supreme Council, which alone has the power to pass laws. Its 111 members are elected for a five-year term by secret ballot and universal suffrage. It elects from among its members the Presidium of between eleven and seventeen members, which serves as its permanent organ. The Presidium's president serves as chief of state. The council similarly elects the prime minister, approves the ministers he appoints, and chooses senior judges and attorneys general. At the provincial and district levels, People's Local Councils are elected for terms of two and one-half years to direct local affairs in the economic, social, and cultural fields in cooperation with the mass organizations, state farms, and the like, and under supervision of the central executive agencies.

In operation, these institutions have produced a relatively well-integrated governing structure, tightly centralized wherever communications with the capital are adequate. In 1971, when the first People's Supreme Council was formed, local organization had not proceeded far enough to make elections feasible, and all members were party appointees. In 1978, however, direct elections were held for the Supreme Council. Candidates were doubtless carefully screened, but membership in the YSP was not made a necessary qualification; 40 of the 111 seats were in fact won by persons who were not party members. The electoral law reserved a bloc of seats for nominees of the General Union of Yemeni Women (GUYW), and women were also free to stand as candidates for elective seats.

The most obvious opposition to the restructuring of South Yemeni society has occurred in the field of female participation in public activities. The GUYW is a 15,000-member organization under firm party guidance. It has been given the task of establishing training schools to educate girls in various clerical, mechanical, and industrial skills, and in 1975, 1,500 women were enrolled in such centers as resident students. Protest by conservative parents, however, forced the closure of the centers in the Fourth and Sixth Governorates in 1978.[11]

THE ARMED FORCES

The Federal Army bequeathed by the old regime had swung, by and large, to the NLF side in the preindependence civil war. Many of its senior officers, however, were firmly oriented toward the traditional tribal structure of South Yemeni society and, as we have seen, opposed the "corrective" changes proposed by the Fourth Congress. The party's left wing agitated for the complete dissolution of the army as a counter-revolutionary and neocolonialist element. This radical measure was rejected in favor of a more gradual, but equally effective, transformation in which guerrilla formations were amalgamated with the regular forces and British-trained officers progressively eliminated. The socialist countries replaced the United Kingdom as the principal source of weapons. The reorganized forces received Soviet and, later, Cuban training. By 1981, the country's military establishment was believed to consist of an army of 22,000 (with a very substantial expansion on the drawing-board), an air force of 1,300, and a small navy of 500, all well armed and well disciplined.

Given the country's limited manpower resources, the regime has found it useful to make rather extensive use of armed forces personnel in civic action, and this principle is sanctioned by the constitution (Article 33). Soldiers contribute substantially to the progress of road and building construction and irrigation works. While party control of the army is unquestioned, factionalism within the YSP has its reflection in the military, and this has played a prominent role in successive party crises.

Supplementing the conventional forces, a people's militia has been organized at the local level whose members receive twenty days' training a year. The force is under the command of a YSP central committee member, Hussein Qumata. It claims to have a total strength approaching 100,000, but this figure is probably quite exaggerated.

NOTES

1. Tareq Ismael, *The Arab Left* (Syracuse, N.Y.: Syracuse University Press, 1976), especially pp. 92–107.

2. Ibid., p. 106.

3. *Azmat al-Thawra fi Janub al-Yaman* [The crisis of the revolution in South Yemen] (Beirut: Dar al-Taliᶜa, 1968).

4. Qahtan was furthermore the only NLF leader to have attained the age of forty.

5. The premiership was shortly entrusted to Faisal al-Shaᶜbi.

6. Those declared elected were the nominees who received the most votes. In descending order these were Khalid Abd al-Aziz, Abdul Fattah Ismail, Salim Rubayᶜ Ali, Salih Muslih, Ali Antar, al-Hajj Salih Baqis, Mahmoud Ushaysh, Said al-Dhalaᶜi, Faisal Abd al-Latif al-Shaᶜbi, and Ali Abd al-ᶜAlim. Qahtan al-Shaᶜbi came in sixteenth, thus theoretically failing of election to the ten-member command; but as president, he could hardly be excluded from its deliberations!

7. It was alleged that the U.S. defense attaché directed the arrests from the headquarters of the South Yemen Army's Sixth Brigade. When this allegation was publicly aired, he was expelled from the country, on March 26. South Yemen severed diplomatic relations with the United States the following year, and official contacts have not been resumed.

8. *Programme of the Unified Political Organisation, The National Front, for the National Democratic Phase of the Revolution* (Nottingham: Russell Press for the PDRY Embassy, London, 1977), p. 14.

9. Ibid.

10. A careful analysis of the available evidence is given by Fred Halliday in "Yemen's Unfinished Revolution," *MERIP*, Vol. 9, no. 8 (October 1979): 16–19.

11. For an interesting discussion of the changing situation of women in South Yemen, see Maxine D. Molyneux, "State Policy and the Position of Women in South Yemen," *Peuples Méditerranéens*, no. 12 (July-September 1980): 33–49.

5

The Economy

Broadly speaking, there are two fundamental geographical factors that exercise decisive influence over the South Yemeni economy. The first of these is its scanty endowment in natural resources. No mineral wealth of commercial significance is known to be present, aside from small, isolated deposits of semiprecious gemstones, rock salt, and limestone and other building materials. Agricultural potential in the highlands is strictly limited by the broken nature of the terrain, which confines farming units to quite small plots, while on the coastal plain cultivation can be successfully conducted only at the few locations where fertile soils are found in conjunction with reliable supplies of water for irrigation, either from subsurface reservoirs or from intermittent streams. Ruins of ancient dams and irrigation works indicate that the country was once far more productive, and the decline is most likely attributable both to dessication of the climate over the past two millennia and to social instability inhibiting sustained, organized economic endeavor. South Yemen's agriculture can cover the minimum needs of its people in essential foodstuffs only in years of exceptionally favorable weather. On balance, it must be considered a food-deficit country.

On the other hand, South Yemen's geographic situation at the mouth of the Red Sea provides the potential for an important role in the commerce between the Indian Ocean basin and the Mediterranean world. Throughout history, Southern Arabia's economic fortunes have fluctuated with broad shifts in the organization of exchanges between these two great regions. When the trade pattern followed the Red Sea route, merchants and seafarers made use of Aden, one of the few fine natural harbors in the area, and South Yemen prospered. When, for political or strategic reasons, the routes shifted to the Persian Gulf or around the Cape of Good Hope, Aden no longer figured prominently in world trade and the country relapsed into poverty.

Thus, the rise of the Abbasid caliphate in the eighth century attracted the bulk of the maritime commerce to Basra, Sindbad's port of legend, and the commerce of Aden, Shihr, and other ports of the South Arabian littoral stagnated. Baghdad, however, soon lost its grip over the empire's outlying provinces; civil unrest, rebellion, and Turkish incursions interfered with orderly trade, which suffered a devastating blow with the Mongol conquest of Iraq in 1258. Meanwhile, the maritime channel again gravitated westward. Under the local Ma'nid and Zuray'id dynasties, commercial ties were strengthened with Fatimid Egypt, and by the middle of the eleventh century Aden had captured from its Persian Gulf rivals a major share of the transit trade, in which pepper and other spices figured as the most valuable commodities.

The Ayyubids, who conquered Yemen in 1173, were intensely concerned with fostering commerce; they fortified Aden so as to protect merchant shipping from pirates based in the Persian Gulf, and instituted orderly, if onerous, civil administration. When the last Ayyubid departed from Yemen, seventy ships were required to load the luxury merchandise he had tricked the local merchants into entrusting to his entourage. The peaceful passage of rule to the Rasulids in 1229 ushered in the era of South Yemen's greatest prosperity, during which Yemen held a virtual monopoly of the flow of merchandise from India, Ceylon, China, and East Asia through the Red Sea to Egypt and the Mediterranean. Agriculture, notably at Abyan and Lahej, flourished under a sophisticated bureaucratic administration, and vast wealth was devoted to the construction of mosques, schools, and other public buildings.

The mid-fifteenth century witnessed the beginning of a gradual and eventually disastrous economic decline. Hormuz and other Persian Gulf emporiums revived and appropriated a share of the oriental trade, while Shihr and Dhofar asserted their independence of the rule of the last Rasulid kings and their Tahirid successors. The Mameluke sultans of Egypt established direct relations with the Indian princes, and increasingly ships sailed direct from the subcontinent to Jidda and other Red Sea ports in Mameluke hands. At the end of the century the Portuguese entered the Indian Ocean. As one tactic for seizing the oriental trade for themselves, the intruders sought to deny entry of shipping into both the Persian Gulf and the Red Sea. Although Aden's admirable defenses provided a haven for Arab and Indian vessels fleeing both Arab and Portuguese piracy, the volume of merchandise handled diminished drastically. South Yemen became a major base for the ultimately unsuccessful Mameluke, and later Ottoman Turkish, resistance to European incursion into the Indian Ocean basin. During the Turkish occupation between 1538 and 1635 Aden's population, between 50,000 and 60,000 under the Rasulids, began to dwindle and many abandoned buildings fell into ruin.

Portuguese capture of the lion's share of the East-West trade coincided with a profound revolution in the South Arabian economy, with the introduction of coffee cultivation in the Yemeni highlands, begun during the Ottoman occupation. From the middle of the fifteenth century the taste for coffee spread from Arabia eastward to Persia and India, northward to Egypt, the Levant, and North Africa, and eventually to Europe, and Yemen was the sole significant supplier until well into the eighteenth century, when production intensified in Indonesia and the West Indies. South Yemen, however, was largely excluded from the accompanying upsurge in regional prosperity. The main producing areas were the highlands of North Yemen, and economics dictated that coffee, a relatively bulky commodity, be shipped principally through the adjacent ports within the Red Sea, notably Mocha, rather than transported over mountain and desert to the more distant Aden. Imported merchandise (principally Indian textiles) naturally gravitated toward those ports, from where it was transshipped northward to Jidda and Suez. Aden became a backwater; its population fell to a mere thousand or so souls by the early nineteenth century. The formerly lucrative caravan trade northward from the Gulf of Aden declined, and South Yemen sank into political fragmentation and economic stagnation, save for a lively seasonal trade with the Horn of Africa on the opposite side of the Red Sea.

THE PREINDEPENDENCE ECONOMY

Although considerations of imperial strategy were the deciding factor in the British seizure of Aden, there were also hopes that it would become an important world trade center comparable to Singapore at the opposite end of the Indian Ocean. The dream in fact became reality, but only slowly, for a variety of political, economic, and technological reasons.

Throughout the British presence, the fact that Aden was a garrison town was a major factor in the regional economy. For the construction of fortifications, barracks, and administrative headquarters large numbers of unskilled laborers were required. In the early years contract labor was imported from India. By the mid-1850s, with somewhat more stable political relations with Aden's hinterland, a community of migrant workers from North Yemen and Somalia began to form and ultimately became the backbone of the settlement's labor force. At first provisioned from Bombay, the garrison soon began to contract locally for the supply of vegetables, dairy products, fruits, and fodder, while livestock shipped from the Somali coast was pastured in Lahej and other adjacent areas until required on the Aden market. These were the remote origins of a very gradual evolution toward the production of cash crops.

The concept of Aden as an imperial "fortress" survived throughout the British occupation, although obscured at times by the absence of an immediate threat and by wrangling between the government of India and the metropolitan authorities over which should foot the bill for the garrison. Assumption of command by the Royal Air Force in the 1920s stimulated construction of a major airport in the Aden enclave, landing strips throughout the protectorate, and roads from Aden to a few remote urban centers. A final burst of construction activity came in the 1950s and early 1960s when Britain, having lost its Suez base and having concluded that the prospective independence of its East African colonies rendered Kenya an unsuitable alternative, moved its Middle East command to Aden. The ink was scarcely dry on large contracts for building housing for servicemen's families when the decision was reached to terminate all British strategic responsibilities east of Suez. A substantially increased supply of urban housing was one British legacy to independent South Yemen's capital.

From the first, contractors for the garrison were Parsi, Persian, and British merchants who immigrated in the wake of the occupation. Their commercial position rapidly and permanently overshadowed that of the native Arab traders dealing in the region's traditional export commodities, such as gums, resins, dyestuffs, hides and skins, pearls, seashells, and ostrich feathers. These exotic goods were of diminishing concern to an industrializing West. South Arabia and Northeast Africa never became major two-way trading partners of Britain. As the nineteenth century progressed it became evident that Aden's economic future, like its past, lay in the transit trade. But to fulfill the role adequately, its port had to adapt to the changing demands of world maritime commerce.

By the time Britain occupied Aden, the revolutionary shift from sail to steam navigation had begun. French and German, as well as British, firms were introducing regularly scheduled mail and passenger service by steam-driven vessels, and the Indian Navy ships stationed in the area to inhibit the slave trade were also coal-fired steamers, although bulk cargo was still carried mainly in large square-rigged sailing ships. Aden's Front Bay, nestled under the ancient town of Crater and guarded by fortifications on Sirah Island as well as the mainland, although admirably adapted to the shipping of an earlier era, was not suited to the newer vessels. It furthermore began silting up within the first decade of the occupation. The coaling station immediately established was installed at Steamer Point on Back Bay. The local merchants began using this more spacious harbor to unload Somali livestock to be sent to the inland pastures and built wharves at the future town of Maᶜalla, which developed into the permanent principal port facility. Aden's governors, often military men preoccupied with the settlement's fortress role, looked askance at this development beyond the main defense perimeter, but the economic imperatives could not be ignored, particularly after

1850, when the government of India passed an act declaring Aden a free port.

The opening of the Suez Canal in 1869 and the completion the following year of an underwater telegraph from India to Europe via Aden opened up possibilities for the development of the entrepôt and bunkering trade that Aden was not yet in a position to exploit fully. Already in the 1850s ships ran aground with increasing frequency in the shallow Back Bay. The construction of progressively larger, faster steamers doomed the sailing ship. But the new vessels often had to anchor outside the Aden harbor to take on coal – an inefficient, expensive operation dangerous in rough weather. In 1881 the India Office granted permission for a coaling station on the island of Perim to a consortium of entrepreneurs and shipping lines seeking not only to obtain better bunkering facilities at the mouth of the Red Sea but furthermore to drive down the prices charged by the London coal brokers and their Aden agents, the large British and Parsi merchant houses.

Thus began a long and bitter trade war that persisted until the shift from coal to oil as bunker fuel. As neither the government of India nor the London authorities were prepared to pay for the dredging of Aden's harbor, the town's initial disadvantage was perforce corrected by vigorous action on the part of its own commercial companies. They managed to secure the establishment of the Port Trust, with business participation, endowed with a substantial accumulation of port dues. With the completion of the first dredging program in 1895 the balance swung decisively in Aden's favor. The trust went forward with further improvements, including land reclamation projects, and thenceforth kept the port fully competitive with its rivals. Provision of oil-bunkering facilities and completion of the British Petroleum refinery in 1954 so enhanced Aden's attractiveness to shipping that by 1958 it had become, after New York, the world's busiest port.

Aden's hinterland was at best marginally and partially involved in this burgeoning economic expansion until the final years of the British presence. Political fragmentation and civil unrest inhibited any sustained effort to expand agricultural production. The ruling chiefs were not "development minded," with the occasional exception of the Abdali sultans, whose loss of the port of Aden forced them to seek other sources of revenue. In the early years the British lent advice and some assistance for expansion of the cultivated area along Wadi Tiban and furnished seeds for the raising of vegetables and fruits for the Aden market. As the British position became consolidated, the source of supply of fodder and other provisions moved further inland, as far as Upper Yafiᶜ. Otherwise, British economic concern in the hinterland was long confined to ensuring the security of the caravan routes by which North Yemeni coffee and other exportable commodities were carried to Aden and endeavoring to keep the transit tolls exacted by the various ruling chiefs along these routes (from which a vital portion of their revenues was derived) at an economic level. At the beginning of the twentieth century, under the forward-looking Curzon governorship of India, a project was conceived for more direct British intervention in Aden's hinterland to institute economic progress, raise living standards, and provide more equitable administration. The notion was firmly vetoed by the government in London, however, and it was not until 1943 that problems of wartime supply, compounded by a severe drought and widespread starvation, brought vigorous action by the Aden regime to expand and modernize the protectorate's economic base.

Particular attention focused on Wadi Bana, a flourishing agricultural district in ancient and medieval times. Astride the border between the Fadli and Lower Yafiᶜ sultanates, its possession had long been in dispute between the two tribal groups, to the detriment of its utilization. In 1938, less than 400 hectares (1,000 acres) were under cultivation out of a total potentially productive area of perhaps 48,000 hectares (120,000 acres).[1] In June 1943, disregarding the proprietary claims of the two rulers, British technicians moved into the area under armed forces protection. Under management of an ad hoc Khanfar Development Board financed by British loans, irrigation works were constructed and an initial 240 hectares (600 acres) allocated to peasants. During its four years of operation the board supervised the reclamation of 2,000 hectares (5,000 acres) of previously unproductive land. Smaller emergency projects were undertaken elsewhere in the protectorate: in Lower Awlaqi, Bayhan, and wherever land and water conditions permitted.

In 1947 the Khanfar scheme was reorganized as the Abyan Development Board, financed by credits of £170,000 from the Colonial Development and Welfare Fund, £90,000 from the British Raw Cotton Commission, and £105,000 from the Aden Colony treasury. The board proceeded to undertake a relatively large, integrated program based on the cultivation of medium-staple cotton, experimental plantings of which had produced encouraging results. After ten years of operation, 20,000 hectares (50,000 acres) had been brought into production, of which an annual average of 12,000 hectares (30,000 acres) was planted in cotton. Ginning and baling machinery was installed, a marketing board organized, and a price stabilization fund established to equalize fluctuations in the world cotton market. Although ownership of the land remained mainly with the rulers and notables, the tenant or sharecropping farmers were assured tenure so long as they followed the board's technical guidance in methods of cultivation and crop rotation and were guaranteed an equitable share in the marketing proceeds. The Abyan district grew to a community of 40,000, equipped with gravel roads, modern housing, running water, and electric power, which was extended to Jaᶜar and Zinjibar, the nearby capitals of the Lower Yafiᶜ and Fadli sultanates.

The commercial success of the Abyan scheme served as an example for progress in other protectorate states, on their own initiative or at the instance of British colonial officials, with both technical and financial support by the Abyan Board. Lahej, the state best favored with fertile land and irrigation water, began cotton production in 1954; by 1960 it was devoting about one-third of its 12,000 cultivated hectares to this crop, employing 3,500 peasants, producing 14,000 bales per year, and ginning its own cotton. Regular, if scattered, plantings on a much smaller scale were introduced in Awdali, Lower Awlaqi, Aqrabi, Dathina, and even at Maifaᶜ in the Eastern Protectorate. On the eve of independence about 22,000 hectares (55,000 acres) – roughly one-third of the country's cultivated area – were planted in cotton, with an annual yield of 35–40,000 bales of cotton and 5–10,000 tons of cottonseed. Until 1957 South Yemen enjoyed a protected market through contracts with the Raw Cotton Commission in Britain. Thereafter it was at the mercy of the volatile world market, in competition with far larger producers. Cotton accounted for more than one-half the protectorate's export earnings, which fluctuated between £1.5 and £2.0 million.

The protectorate did not, of course, constitute an integrated economic unit, and this fact had political repercussions. A certain percentage was deducted from the share of export earnings attributable to the Abyan cotton farmers to finance the Abyan Board's price stabilization fund, debt amortization, and infrastructural programs. This was resented by the peasants, particularly as in Lahej the farmer was paid his full share on a current basis. The colonial power, needless to say, was blamed for the disparity (see Chapter 3).

The development directed, and largely financed, by the British was inevitably accompanied by some social dislocation and political unrest. In some of the more primitive areas it actually deprived some citizens of their age-old sources of livelihood. Along the mountainous routes from North Yemen and Hadramawt to the Gulf of Aden caravans had customarily employed guides from the successive tribes along the way and paid them transit dues. Many tribesmen furthermore lived by raising camels and hiring them for transport. As motorable roads were built by the British toward the more remote parts of the protectorate (primarily for military purposes), small entrepreneurs, principally from Aden, began to introduce the carriage of freight by truck and sought to avoid any payment to the tribes en route. The British authorities endeavored to rationalize the situation provisionally by forbidding the carriage of cer-

tain commodities by motor vehicle while tolerating the collection of
tolls. Trucking nevertheless flourished, accompanied by increased civil
disobedience and banditry on the roads. This situation was most serious
in resource-poor areas such as Radfan, where the tribes were nominal
subjects of the Dali amirate but in fact answered to no outside authority. A parallel development occurred in the Eastern Protectorate, where
citizens who had enriched themselves in southeastern Asia took the initiative in constructing motor roads from the coast inland to Wadi
Hadramawt, threatening the livelihood of the tribes on the *jol*, the intervening desert plateau.

After the mid-1950s Britain, having suffered serious reverses in its
Middle Eastern policies and faced with mounting armed opposition to its
rule in South Yemen, largely abandoned further development programs.
Its efforts had appreciably expanded the country's overall economic
base. Only minor progress had been achieved, however, toward knitting
the scattered pockets of new wealth-producing enterprise into a single,
integrated economy. The Aden enclave was firmly oriented toward the
world of international commerce and British imperial strategy, while the
protectorate's economic links with the outside, save for the cotton
market, were few and in the case of Hadramawt, had actually declined.
The welfare of the farmers who manned the commercial agricultural
projects had undoubtedly improved, but the disparity between their condition and that of the princes who retained ownership of the land actually widened. Increased prosperity in Abyan or Lahej brought no
benefit to the nomad herdsmen or the peasants tilling tiny terraced plots
in the uplands. Political dissent was rooted only partly in economic
discontent, but there can be no doubt that perceived inequities contributed to the triumph of revolutionary economic policies after South
Yemen became independent.

THE ECONOMY SINCE INDEPENDENCE

After a few years of chaos and improvisation, the NLF set about
transforming the character of South Yemen's economy, in the face of
considerable obstacles. British budget support in Aden and the federation, which had amounted to an annual £14 million, ceased abruptly,
along with the local expenditures of the British garrison, which had produced an equivalent amount in foreign exchange. The modern sector,
mostly foreign-owned, was acutely depressed by civil unrest and, more
particularly, by the closure of the Suez Canal in the June 1967 Arab-
Israeli war. The new national leadership was oriented from the outset
toward a socialized economy. Coherent theory and specific objectives
took several years to crystallize and were the object of contention among

various factions within the NLF – communist, Maoist, Baathist, and Arab nationalist. But it was a "scientific" socialism deeply influenced by Soviet thinking that won out over nationalist and Maoist trends. By the mid-1970s the PDRY's economic aims were clear: to concentrate the means of production and distribution in the hands of the state; to shift the basis of the economy from services to production; to develop a resource and technological base; to ensure an equitable distribution of income; and to provide for essential human social needs.

Under the Economic Organization Law enacted in 1969 the country's eight banks (all but one of which were foreign-owned) were taken over and amalgamated into the National Bank of Yemen. Insurance firms were liquidated or consolidated in the public-sector Insurance and Reinsurance Company. The major trading concerns were expropriated and organized into the National Corporation for Foreign Trade and the National Home Trade Company. The companies providing services (except oil bunkering) to the port of Aden were nationalized and placed under the Ports Board. Petroleum distribution companies were seized and their functions entrusted to the Petroleum Board. In 1977, control of the Aden refinery, already amortized on British Petroleum's books, was transferred by mutual consent to the PDRY government. When, in the following year, the cable and wireless telecommunications installations were similarly taken over, the only foreign firms operating in the country were several international oil companies providing bunker fuel in Aden port.

Meanwhile, the traditional productive sectors were drastically restructured. Agricultural lands were confiscated from the former rulers and other absentee landowners. By 1972, arable land had been organized into state farms or into cooperatives. Marketing and the supply of services were concentrated in the hands of government agencies. Fishing boats and gear were nationalized and distribution of the catch was placed under the control of a cooperative. Similar collectivization was applied to traditional handicrafts and to retail trade. All housing was nationalized, with the single exception of owner-occupied dwellings. The results of government management of virtually all economic activity have been mixed, as a brief review of the various sectors will show.

AGRICULTURE

South Yemen's agricultural potential is limited by rugged terrain, scarcity of suitable soils, and a meager, uncertain supply of water. Of the country's total area only an estimated 80,000 hectares (200,000 acres) are arable, and of these not much more than 60 percent are cultivated in a given year. Semidesert rangelands are extensive but sparsely vegetated, and watering points are widely dispersed. About 70 percent of the population, including the stock-raising nomads, lives in rural areas, and the sector employs more than 40 percent of the labor force. As of 1978, however, crop production accounted for only 7 percent of gross domestic product (GDP) and fell far short of meeting the country's minimum needs. PDRY imports all its tea, sugar, and rice requirements, 50 percent of its maize, 75 percent of its wheat, and 45 percent of its meat and vegetables, at a cost of about YD25 million annually.[2]

Between 1971 and 1977 the government invested YD34 million – 22 percent of its development outlays – in the agricultural sector. That the results in terms of production were disappointing is due to a number of factors: the difficulty of adapting to the new institutions, faulty management, and some sheer bad luck. Under the new agricultural structure about 12,000 hectares (30,000 acres), including the Abyan and Lahej areas where some modern technology had been introduced before independence, were confiscated and organized as state farms on which the peasants work as wage earners. The remaining cultivated land, save for a few plots in remote areas, was organized into cooperatives of two types: "production sharing," where the land is worked in common and the income distributed pro rata; and "service sharing," where individuals till their own holdings but share the costs of inputs such as machinery, fertilizer, and pesticides. Cropping patterns are imposed by central planners, and marketing – at fixed prices – is a state monopoly. Peasants are permitted to own poultry, sheep, and goats, although any surplus must be sold through the established state agencies. About one-third of the country's livestock remains in the hands of the Bedouin. Although a much-needed well-drilling program has been conducted with UN assistance, livestock is still vulnerable to climatic vagaries; in the late 1970s the nomads' flocks were decimated by drought. With Cuban help a large poultry-raising complex was constructed, but the project suffered a severe setback in 1978, when nearly the entire flock was wiped out by disease.

Productivity of the individual farmer is an acute and unsolved problem. On the state farms, where the peasants are paid the minimum wage, a study by the Food and Agriculture Organization showed that they were working less than four hours a day. The system of fixed prices and imposed crop patterns results in sharp fluctuations in the return on land farmed cooperatively. Under the production sharing system there is little close relationship between individual effort and income. Such a relationship is rather more evident in the service-sharing cooperatives, which a 1977 World Bank survey found to be the most efficient of the new agricultural institutions. Nevertheless, the government intended to place all cooperatives on the production-sharing basis by 1982, appar-

Table 1:   Agricultural Production
(thousands of metric tons)

	1969/70	1972/73	1973/74	1974/75	1975/76	1976/77
Cotton	12.8	13.2	10.3	10.8	9.3	4.9
Sesame	3.4	3.4	1.2	2.0	1.7	2.9
Coffee	0.8	0.8	0.8	0.8	0.8	0.8
Tobacco	1.4	1.4	1.2	1.2	1.2	1.2
Wheat	12.0	12.5	9.0	10.0	10.0	9.1

Source: People's Democratic Republic of Yemen: A Review of
Economic and Social Development (Washington: The
World Bank, 1979) p. 28.

ently to eliminate the remaining vestiges of private ownership of the
means of production. There have been serious shortcomings in providing
the agricultural inputs for which central authority has assumed responsibility, and considerable waste and loss in handling and storage. World
Bank figures showed a decline since independence in the production of
major crops (Table 1). The fall in cotton production is attributable in part
to a shift from cotton growing to producing grain, fruit, and vegetables.
Nevertheless, overall agricultural production clearly appears to have
fallen since preindependence days, and serious problems must be solved
if South Yemen's dependence on foreign sources of food is to be reduced.

FISHERIES

South Yemen's coastal waters are rich in a variety of vertebrate fish
and crustaceans. Until independence, fishing provided a livelihood for
about 13,000 private fishermen. In the absence of cold storage and transport facilties, the catch furnished food only for the inhabitants of the
coastal towns and villages. Much of it was dried on the beaches and carried inland by camel caravan for use as livestock feed and fertilizer.
Under the 1969 nationalization law, fishing craft and implements were
collectivized and the fishermen organized into fourteen cooperatives
under the Ministry of Fish Wealth. Between 1971 and 1977, YD22.8
million, or 14 percent of the PDRY development effort, was invested in
fisheries. Objectives of the program were to establish central control of
the sector, to distribute the product efficiently throughout the country so
as to reduce the necessity of food imports, and to increase export earn-

ings. The ministry has acquired a modern fishing fleet, which it operates primarily for the export market, and is engaged in a joint venture with the USSR, also for export. A Japanese firm, Nichiro, holds a concession, principally for cuttlefish, on a royalty basis, from which the PDRY received YD2.6 million in 1976.

Although the cooperatives branch of the industry has been somewhat neglected and the domestic distribution system needs further improvement, much has been achieved in the fisheries industry. In 1976 it accounted for a production valued at YD15.6 million, significantly more than the combined product of agriculture and stock raising (YD14.3 million). In 1977 fish and fish meal constituted 59 percent of the country's commodity exports, earning YD5.9 million in foreign exchange. As it is estimated that the 1976 production of commercially valuable fish (160,000 metric tons, or 186,000 short tons) was less than one-third of the sustainable yield, there is clearly room for considerable future expansion.

INDUSTRY

Given South Yemen's narrow resource base, the absence of known mineral wealth, and the small domestic market, the country's industrial potential is quite limited. Aside from the Aden refinery discussed below, manufacturing has necessarily emphasized the processing of agricultural products. The regime has sought to expand the state's role in industry. During the first two development plan periods (1971–1979), major projects included a textile factory of 7.2 million yards (6.5 million meters) annual capacity built by the People's Republic of China, a flour mill (56,000 metric tons, or 62,000 short tons capacity), a tomato paste cannery, and a dairy products factory. Cement, glass, and additional canning factories are in prospect for the near future.

The regime has not assumed actual ownership of the enterprises, mostly quite small, that were in operation or under construction when the 1971 Investment Law was placed in effect. The private sector is encouraged to join in mixed ventures with the state, and this sector has shown substantial growth. Expatriate Yemeni workers constitute a large potential source of investment funds for the mixed sector, the exploitation of which will depend on appropriate guarantees by the government.

THE ADEN REFINERY

This installation, which employed 1,800 workers in 1978, was completed in 1954 by British Petroleum (BP) with an annual capacity of 8.5 million metric tons (9.4 million short tons). It operates by the now obsolescent hydro-skimming process (which yields a smaller proportion of high distillates than more modern methods), and its aging equipment will require substantial capital investment for profitable operation. When the PDRY assumed control of the plant in May 1977, the closure of the Suez Canal, development of more efficient refining processes in Europe and elsewhere, and the altered pattern of world shipping had led BP to reduce its Aden production to 1.6 million metric tons (1.8 million short tons) annually. Under Yemeni management throughput has risen only modestly, for both technical and political reasons. Marketing complexities make it excessively speculative for Aden to purchase and process crude oil and to export the refined products for its own account. Most of its operations take the form of processing crude bought by Third World countries lacking refining facilities of their own, at a fee of US $1 per barrel. In 1978 certain crude oil producers, at odds with the political orientation of the PDRY government, declined to sell crude for processing at Aden. In 1979, production was 1.8 million metric tons (2 million short tons), including processing one-half million tons each for Libya and Kuwait and a similar amount of Soviet crude, mainly for the local market. In 1980, a contract for 1 million tons was signed for the account of India, where civil unrest had closed down some refineries. This brought the production rate to 2.8 million metric tons (3.1 million short tons), well below the estimated break-even point of 3.4 million metric tons (3.7 million short tons). Substantially increased production furthermore depends on the provision of deep-water mooring facilities for large tankers, which cannot enter Aden harbor, and additional storage capacity.

Procurement and distribution of petroleum products for local consumption is administered by the Yemeni National Oil Company. Bunkering at Aden port, however, remains in the hands of several international oil companies. The latter purchase no more than half their requirements from the Aden refinery, whose prices are not competitive with the cost of fuels imported from the companies' own refineries elsewhere.

ADEN PORT

The PDRY has centralized all operations in Aden Port under the Yemen Ports and Shipping Corporation, which supervises three subsidiaries responsible respectively for port operations, for stevedoring, shipping, and shipping agency activities, and for ship repairing. Overall port activities have recovered only partially from the dramatic decline following the closure of the Suez Canal in 1967. The port nevertheless remains a vital economic asset whose foreign exchange earnings, estimated

Table 2:   Activity in Aden Port
(thousand long tons)

	1966	1969	1973	1976	1977
Number of ships	6,246	1,568	1,320	2,336	2,605
Net registered tonnage	31,425	8,089	5,565	9,944	10,738
Dry cargo imported	647	406	312	387	618
Dry cargo exported	184	99	65	80	79
Oil imports	8,072	6,068	3,342	1,779	1,811
Oil exports	3,985	5,584	2,724	1,311	1,294
Oil bunkers	3,486	387	388	638	658
Transit passengers	146,300	2,519	...	...	...

Source: People's Democratic Republic of Yemen, p. 39.

at between US $15 and US $20 million in 1978, may be expected to grow.

In order to take advantage of the reopening of the Suez Canal in June 1975, the South Yemeni government refurbished the port at a cost of about US $18 million with the assistance of the International Development Association and the Arab Fund for Economic and Social Development. Traffic increased significantly, but less than had been anticipated. Shipping patterns had changed. A large proportion of Persian Gulf oil was now carried in supertankers that could not transit the Suez Canal fully loaded and therefore followed the Cape of Good Hope route. Competition for bunkering had intensified from other ports in the region, notably Jidda. A sharp increase in dry cargo imports mainly reflects South Yemen's own rising import needs and transit trade to North Yemen, whose port of Hodeida is chronically congested.

Seeking to enhance the port's earning capacity, South Yemen has purchased a floating drydock from Japan. Berths equipped with cargo-handling gear are being provided to supplement lighterage. Expansion of the small remaining tax-free enclave in the port is under consideration as a means of revitalizing the entrepôt trade.

SOCIAL DEVELOPMENT

At independence, South Yemen faced grave social problems and imbalances. Barely 18 percent of the population was literate. Productive assets were owned by a small minority of rulers, tribal chiefs, and foreigners. The vast majority of the people outside Aden lived in poverty, particularly acute among the Bedouin in the northern regions. Medical services were totally lacking in the former protectorate states, schools were few, housing substandard, and nutrition inadequate. In Aden itself, there was much unemployment due to the decline in shipping and commercial activity during the final years of the British presence. Although the British left a substantial stock of housing recently built for their military forces and dependents, it deteriorated rapidly for lack of maintenance, and a housing shortage soon developed. The exodus of indigenous, as well as immigrant, workers left many gaps in the work force, and by 1973 an actual labor shortage had appeared—a rare phenomenon in a developing country. The PDRY government has given close attention to these various issues.

Particular effort has been exerted in the field of education at all levels. A crash program patterned after the Cuban model to reduce adult illiteracy produced somewhat disappointing results (the available teachers were too few and the population too dispersed); nevertheless, more than 73,000 Yemenis had completed literacy courses by 1977, and the program has been continued. At independence, 64,500 Yemenis were in schools; in 1979 there were more than a quarter of a million—one of every seven residents. Education has been extended throughout the countryside. Boarding schools have been established for the children of Bedouin families. The new comprehensive system of primary and secondary schools has been capped by a university with five faculties and an enrollment that rose from 362 in 1970 to nearly 1,700 in 1977. South Yemen's commitment to education is reflected in its expenditure in the mid-1970s of 7.4 percent of GDP in this field, as compared with an average of 4.4 percent for all less developed countries.

Strong emphasis has been placed on science and engineering. A British school, opened in the 1950s to train skilled workmen for the port and refinery, has been developed into an integrated College of Technology, with advice and equipment from the United Nations Educational, Scientific and Cultural Organization (UNESCO). In 1979 it had 250 students in night-school crafts courses, 700 at the lower-technician level, and 560 at the engineering level, of whom 75 were permitted to go on for master's degrees. Qualified Yemenis are gradually replacing the Russian and Indian faculty. Instruction is in English.

The special effort made to provide equal education for girls is part of South Yemen's policy of emancipating women and recruiting them into the nation's labor force. Legislation introduced in 1974 prohibits polygamy and child marriages and otherwise moves toward placing men and women on an equal legal basis. The notion of female employment, of course, was not completely innovative. In the poverty-stricken rural areas a family could survive only if more than one of its members worked, and women made up nearly one-third of the agricultural work force. Training programs have more recently brought considerable numbers of women into urban jobs as accountants, factory workers, mechanics, tractor drivers, and the like, which were formerly restricted to males. The program has been criticized by the governments of the PDRY's conservative neighbors, and it has met with considerable local opposition from those faithful to the traditional Islamic concepts of women's social role. The emancipation process is by no means complete, but South Yemen has gone much further in this direction than any other Arabian Peninsula country.

REDISTRIBUTION OF INCOME

In addition to assuming control of the country's productive assets, the regime has moved to equalize the remuneration of its employees, totaling some 150,000, or well over one-third of the labor force. Under the preindependence government pay scale, the highest-paid worker received eleven times the wage of the lowest-paid; the ratio now stands at 3.5 to 1. The income of private individuals is taxed twice. A sharply progressive special tax is applied, rising to 37.5 percent on annual incomes above YD900 and 47.5 percent above YD2,400. The remainder is subject to the general income tax, itself also progressive. The result, in the judgment of the 1977 World Bank team, is among the world's most egalitarian systems for the distribution of domestically earned income.[3]

Sharp disparities nevertheless remain, the most serious being that between urban dwellers and the people dependent upon agriculture and fishing. The dispersion of the population is suggested by estimates of the population of the principal towns, shown in Table 3. The average income per capita among the 180,000 workers employed in agriculture and fishing is less than half the national average, although absolute poverty is less widespread than in the preindependence era. Improvement of the communications network has increased the government's ability to deliver food and services such as medical care and education in outlying regions. The completion of a paved coastal road between Aden and Mukalla, for example, has made it possible for fishermen to market a far larger proportion of their catch as "wet" fish for human consumption. Nevertheless, the great majority of the rural population lacks adequate shelter, sewage, pure water, and electricity, and nutrition is believed to be substandard. In the late 1970s the problem led the regime to give serious consideration to a plan to resettle the entire rural population in twenty-two fishery centers and fifty-four agricultural communities. This would not of itself solve the problem of low productivity, which is more

Table 3:   Population of Principal Towns

	1973 Census	1977 Estimate
Aden	240,372	271,593
Mukalla	44,626	50,422
Saywun	19,248	21,748
Shihr	17,291	19,537
Tarim	17,094	19,314
Al-Hawta (Lahej)	14,029	15,851
Ja 'ar	10,488	11,850

Source: Ministry of Information, People's Democratic Republic of Yemen, Statistical Glimpse (Aden, 1977?)

closely related to that of creating incentives in a socialized economy.

A further element in the income-distribution pattern is the large proportion of South Yemenis working abroad. As much as one-third of the entire labor force is outside the country; the number of migrants was estimated at 125,000 in 1976. In 1973, when labor shortages began to appear, the government prohibited further emigration. There can be little doubt that the exodus would resume on a large scale if the restriction were relaxed, in view of the lucrative employment opportunities available in the nearby oil-producing countries. Remittances from the expatriates were estimated at US $57 million in 1969. During the period of transition to socialism they dropped appreciably (to US $33 million in 1973). As domestic stability was established and the new order became more or less accepted, they increased rapidly, reaching US $180 million in 1977 — by far the country's largest source of foreign exchange. The transfers accrue to private individuals, usually relatives of the migrant workers. They greatly enhance the PDRY's ability to import the commodities it needs. The country's leaders are aware, at the same time, that if measures were taken to mobilize the funds for public-sector investment the flow would soon dry up. They have therefore been careful to preserve confidence by permitting reconversion to foreign currencies, providing preferential interest rates, allowing duty-free import of accompanied articles, and allowing the funds to be used for construction of owner-occupied housing.

The issue of migrant labor is a complex one with some adverse aspects. There is no prospect that the expatriates will return to South Yemen until their working lives are over; the skills they acquire will therefore not be of direct benefit to the country's own development. If the ban on emigration continues, the flow of remittances will eventually decline and finally cease. Meanwhile, some recipients – chiefly women and children but also males of working age – find it possible to meet their needs without working.

NATIONAL ACCOUNTS

As previously noted, South Yemen's preindependence economy was quite fragmented. Public finances were dispersed among the federal government, Aden Colony, and the various princely states, of which fifteen had conventional budgets and responsible accounting services. At all levels British budgetary support was of critical importance. Accurate figures for the region's gross domestic product for this period are lacking, but it is believed to have fallen by 20 percent between 1966 and 1968. The tightly centralized institutions introduced by the Corrective Movement after 1969 produced a sharp reorientation of the economy from services to investment in productive facilities. As a result, a sustained growth rate of about 7 percent was achieved by the middle and late 1970s. After 1973, remittances by emigrant workers exceeded by far the former British subsidy. Remittances constituted 30 percent of gross national product by 1977 and were equivalent to a whopping 40 percent of GDP. These foreign exchange receipts have allowed the import of commodities for consumption and substantial capital-development goods while preserving a fairly strong balance-of-payments position. The economy nevertheless remained in deep deficit at the rate of expenditure recorded in the early 1980s.

South Yemen has consistently run a budget deficit exceeding its total domestic revenues. The shortfall has been covered by external aid and, to a lesser extent, by borrowing from the banking system. The availability of grant and loan assistance from abroad is a critical factor in the level of expenditure and thus the pace of development. The regime has exhibited some restraint in the proportion of resources devoted to defense, which decreased from 48.8 percent of total disbursements in FY 1969-1970 to 18.6 percent in FY 1977.[4] Over the same period economic development expenditures rose from 40.47 percent to 56.2 percent, representing a cumulative investment of more than YD161 million.

By nearly any measure, South Yemen in the 1980s is among the world's poorest countries. Earlier in this chapter we saw that the periods of prosperity it knew in the past depended upon its role as entrepôt and as middleman in international trade. Its indigenous products, notably the

Table 4:   Balance of Payments
(US$ million)

	1969	1973	1975	1976	1977
Domestic Exports, f.o.b.	8	14	8	26	29
Retained Imports, c.i.f.	-87	-120	-165	-267	-324
Trade Deficit	-79	-106	-157	-241	-295
Invisibles, net	80	54	76	145	205
Workers Remittances	57	33	56	115	180
Others	23	21	20	30	25
Balance on Goods and Services	1	-52	-81	-95	-90
Official Transfers	1	...	10	46	55
Official Loan Capital, net	5	25	31	58	68
Gross disbursement	5	25	32	60	69
Repayments	...	...	-1	-2	-1
Miscellaneous capital, net	-13	23	16	-21	7
Overall Balance	-6	-4	-24	-13	40

Source: People's Democratic Republic of Yemen, p. 21.

aromatics that figured prominently in the ancient world's commerce, have lost any significance. Long past, similarly, are the frequent calls by passenger ships, once a distinctive feature of Adeni life and a stimulus to its retail trade. The carriage of crude oil from the Persian Gulf to the industrialized countries is now preponderant in Indian Ocean maritime traffic. With the shift to deep-draft supertankers after the 1967 closure of the Suez Canal, the principal shipping routes have moved far to the south, bypassing Aden. Egypt's completion of the Sumed oil pipeline between the Red Sea and the Mediterranean will doubtless divert a part of the petroleum flow back to the old route; but Aden can aspire to a substantial share in servicing this shipping only by large capital expenditures to improve its facilities and by successful competition with rival developing ports such as Jidda and Yenbo.

A broad assessment of South Yemen's economy before and after independence must include some observations that do not emerge from bare figures. The building of Aden under British auspices from a nearly deserted village to a thriving, modern metropolis integrated with the vast networks of international commerce brought prosperity to only a tiny minority of native South Yemenis. The principal beneficiaries were foreigners: British multinational trading, shipping, engineering, and oil firms; merchants and retailers from the Indian subcontinent and other parts of the empire; and even the North Yemenis and Somalis who composed the backbone of the modernized sector's labor force. Little or none of Aden's wealth trickled into the hinterland. Such development as took place there (mainly growing cotton) was chiefly on British initiative; although the peasants participating in these projects gained in economic security, the land they tilled was owned by the *dawlas* and other elites who were politically compromised by their identification with the protecting power. The latter's efforts to ensure public order and modern, secure channels of distribution were unimpeachably justified by standards prevailing elsewhere; but in South Yemen they had the entirely unintended result of depriving large numbers of South Yemeni tribesmen of their traditional sources of livelihood. These considerations help to explain why the new leadership, itself drawn from the disadvantaged classes, was able to mobilize mass support for loosening the country's links with world commerce and for restructuring the economy on new bases.

The expansion of South Yemen's productive capacity so as to achieve a self-sustaining economy will be a difficult, protracted task at best, and probably impossible without liberal financial and technological help from outside. Maximization of external assistance, however, has thus far been subordinated to other ideological objectives, as will be seen in the concluding chapter's discussion of South Yemen's foreign relations.

NOTES

1. Muhammad ʿUmar al-Habashi, *L'Evolution politique, économique et sociale de l'Arabie du Sud* [The political, economic, and social evolution of South Arabia] (Algiers: Société Nationale d'Edition et de Diffusion, 1966), p. 182.

2. The PDRY's monetary unit, the Yemeni dinar, was quoted at US$2.92 in 1977 and US$2.95 in 1981.

3. *People's Democratic Republic of Yemen: A Review of Economic and Social Development* (Washington, D.C.: World Bank, 1979), p. 41.

4. The South Yemen fiscal year was April 1–March 31 until 1975, when it was placed on a calendar-year basis.

6

South Yemen on the International Scene

In its external relations, the South Yemeni regime's orientation is based on the familiar Marxist assumption that the present phase of world history is that of the decline of imperialism, neocolonialism, and capitalism and of the ascendancy of popular liberation movements that will culminate in the final global victory of peace, democracy, and socialism. As expressed in the program adopted at the Unification Congress of 1975,[1] the ruling party considers South Yemen's revolution as one achievement in this universal process and conceives foreign policy objectives in terms of contributing to its further advance. Thus, at the level of the Arab world the party seeks to combine all progressive and revolutionary Arabs in a single movement that will expel colonial military bases; end the dominance of monopoly capitalist companies; overthrow reactionary Arab regimes; and promote the unity of the Palestinian Arabs within the framework of the Palestine Liberation Organization (PLO) in order to bring down the Zionist regime (perceived as a settler colonialist one), restore the legitimate rights of the Palestinians, and recover Arab territory occupied in the 1967 war.

On the broader world scene, specific support is expressed for the strengthening of the national independence of Vietnam and Indochina; for the struggles of the Latin American peoples, spearheaded by Cuba, which has "built socialism on the doorstep of the leading imperialist nation;" and for the liberation of South Korea from U.S. imperialism and the consequent unification of the Korean nation. Imperialism is declared to bear responsibility for both world wars and, under U.S. leadership, for the current threat of nuclear war, the overthrow of progressive regimes by armed force, obstruction of national liberation movements, and efforts to deny peoples' rights to freedom, national independence, and self-determination. Seeing in the socialist camp, in the international working class and its vanguard parties, and in national liberation movements throughout the world the principal contemporary historical forces, the party seeks to strive for unity among these forces and to establish the strongest brotherly relations with all socialist countries.

This formulation of South Yemen's outlook in foreign relations generally confirmed a pattern established in practice over the preceding eight years, notwithstanding occasional disputes among the South Yemeni leaders in which ideology proved a stronger deciding factor than what some might consider the country's material interests. At independence, the NLF had no friends among the Middle Eastern governments. It was soon at swords' points with its immediate neighbors. Its professedly Marxist radicalism, of a quite different quality from Baathism, Nasserist Arab socialism, and other forms of Arab revolutionary ideology, tended to deter support and cooperation from the "progressive" Arab regimes. The acrimony and violence accompanying the severance of ties with the former colonial power cost the new regime the sympathy of the Western democracies. Its early resort to the cultivation of close links with the Soviet bloc was a matter both of doctrinal compatibility and of survival. The association has, in all likelihood, passed beyond the point where it could be dissolved even in favor of such a major national objective as union with North Yemen.

YEMEN ARAB REPUBLIC

As shown in Chapter 2, geographical Yemen has only rarely constituted a single political unit. A mystique of Yemeni unity nevertheless has arisen within the general context of Arab nationalism and pan-Arabism, by which amalgamation of the two Yemens is seen as a necessary and desirable step toward unification of the entire Arab nation. The concept is enshrined as a major goal in the constitutions of both countries. The preamble to the South Yemeni constitution interprets the revolutions of September 1962 in North Yemen and of October 1963 in the South as aspects of the struggle of a single Yemeni people for freedom and democracy. Article 2 asserts the claim of the Yemeni Socialist Party to leadership of the entire nation:

> The Yemeni people is one people and it is part of the Arab nation and the Yemeni nationality is one. The Yemen constitutes a historical, economical and geographical unity.
> The Yemeni Socialist Party, armed with the Scientific Socialism theory, is the leader and guide of the society and the state. It shall define the general horizon for the development of the society and the line of the state's internal and external policy.

In North Yemen, however, the overthrow of the Zaidi imamate in 1962 did not lead to sweeping social and economic reorganization.

Dissatisfaction persisted, particularly among the Shafeis adjacent to the PDRY, to whom socialist ideas and slogans have considerable appeal. Preponderant power, however, remained with the leaders of major Zaidi tribes and the landed educated elites. Successive Yemen Arab Republic (YAR) governments followed more or less progressive policies, but these remained squarely within the framework of Arab nationalism and solidarity, and strict nonalignment in international affairs. There was little common ground between the respective terms in which North and South Yemen sought union, and the relations between the two were stormy. The first several years of South Yemen's independence were marked by its government's unconcealed support of leftist opposition elements in the North and by retaliatory incursions across the border by YAR forces.

The differences came to a head after 1970, when a national reconciliation in the North under Saudi auspices ended that country's protracted civil war and when the South's Corrective Movement had set it firmly on a socialist path. By mid-1972, serious clashes between the two countries were occurring along the frontier. South Yemeni forces entered Northern territory and executed some forty fugitive Southern tribal chiefs. The Southerners accused the North of invading their territory and threatened retaliatory action by the USSR. The YAR garrisoned Kamaran Island, offshore from its port of Salif but claimed by the PDRY because it had been occupied by Britain and administered by the governor of Aden under the colonial regime. The PDRY accused the YAR and Saudi Arabia of conspiring to seize the island of Perim.

. Following Kuwaiti attempts at mediation, the Arab League addressed the dispute at its Cairo meeting in September 1972 and persuaded the contending parties to a cease-fire and normalization of relations. This was followed up vigorously by Algeria and Libya, who invited the two Yemeni presidents, Salim Rubayᶜ Ali and Abd al-Rahman al-Iryani, to meet at Tripoli in November. A detailed agreement was concluded providing for the establishment of joint committees to negotiate the terms of a full merger between the two Yemens. Algerian and Libyan economic aid to both parties was made conditional on their good faith in the conduct of the negotiations. The committees were promptly organized and began their work.

South Yemen nevertheless intensified its efforts to subvert the YAR regime, as was made publicly clear in the summer of 1973. Dozens of North Yemenis were brought to trial in Sanaa on charges of sabotage and terrorism, for which they acknowledged they had been trained, armed, and paid in South Yemen. Unity negotiations were temporarily suspended after May 20, when a member of the YAR Presidency Council, Shaikh Muhammad Ali Uthman, was assassinated, presumably at PDRY instigation. The committee discussions resumed against a background of rising tension. At the outbreak of the Arab-Israeli war in October the armies of both countries were massed along the border. In the ambient atmosphere of regional crisis, Prime Minister Ali Nasser Muhammad announced that South Yemeni forces had been pulled back from the frontier and called upon North Yemen to reciprocate. Tension eased somewhat, and in May 1974 the two governments instituted joint discussions on sovereignty over the Red Sea islands and other territorial issues.

The military regime that assumed control of North Yemen in June 1974 under Colonel Ibrahim al-Hamdi endeavored to establish a more stable relationship with South Yemen. This entailed placing some distance between the YAR and Saudi Arabia, which had exploited its influence among the powerful Zaidi tribal chiefs to encourage hostility between the two Yemens in order that the YAR might serve as an effective shield for the Saudi kingdom against subversion from South Yemen. Al-Hamdi held a series of meetings with South Yemeni ministers, invited President Salim Rubay⁽ᶜ⁾ Ali on an official visit, and breathed new life into the work of the joint unification committees. Before the end of the year, representatives of the two countries conducted a comprehensive review of the unity discussions with officials of the Arab League, Libya, and Algeria. Meanwhile al-Hamdi, in an effort to remove the sources of discontent in his country's southern areas, appointed a native of the region, Lt. Col. Abdullah Abd al-Alim, to command YAR troops in the area and supervise the local administration. Although the border remained uneasy, these measures, with South Yemen's cooperation at the official level, produced a distinctly healthier atmosphere. In October 1977, however, al-Hamdi fell victim to assassination. While the authors of the deed were never identified and their motives are not known with certainty, it was widely assumed that it was directed against al-Hamdi's policy of accommodation with South Yemen. Abd al-Alim, holding al-Hamdi's successor, Major Ahmad Hussein al-Ghashmi, responsible for the murder, entered upon an unsuccessful armed revolt against the new junta and defected to South Yemen with a number of his troops in May 1978.

The Ghashmi regime retreated from its predecessor's policies of rapprochement with the South and of curbing Saudi influence. Inter-Yemeni relations again rapidly deteriorated. They reached flash point in barely nine months. On June 24, 1978, Ghashmi was killed by a bomb concealed in a briefcase purportedly containing a message from President Salim Rubay⁽ᶜ⁾ Ali. The envoy carrying the message also succumbed to the explosion. The South Yemeni president had publicly expressed his determination to avenge al-Hamdi's murder. No evidence was ever made public, however, that he himself engineered the attack against the North Yemeni leader. The possibility that others planned the deed in order to discredit Salim Rubayᶜ is made plausible by the fact that the incident, and the accompanying new crisis in relations between the two Yemens, occurred at a moment of severe tension within the South Yemeni leadership, over both domestic and foreign policies.

The country had recently embarked on a relatively flexible external policy, expressed in its forthcoming posture toward the al-Hamdi regime, in the opening of diplomatic relations with Saudi Arabia, and in sending out feelers toward the resumption of relations with the United States, broken in 1969 (a middle-rank U.S. diplomat was in fact on his way to Aden when al-Hamdi was killed). These moves had been approved by the South Yemeni collective leadership, although the president's rivals criticized his handling of them. The Ghashmi murder touched off the brief civil war in South Yemen in which Rubayᶜ Ali was deposed and killed and Abdul Fattah Ismail's faction assumed control. Speculative reports in the Cairo press suggested that Ismail and other "pro-Moscow" figures had planned Ghashmi's assassination, blamed it on the fallen president, and executed him to ensure his silence. However this may be, fifteen Arab League states of moderate complexion met on July 2 and declared the suspension of political, economic, and cultural exchanges with South Yemen.[2] This action was ignored by the "progressive" Arab states and thus had minimal practical effect.

Under Ghashmi's successor, Ali Abdullah Salih, repression of dissidence in North Yemen intensified for a time, notably in the border provinces of Taiz and Bayda. Defections to South Yemen multiplied. The dissidents were organized in the National Democratic Front (NDF), a composite of North Yemeni nationalist and leftist elements formed in 1976, headquartered in Aden, which had sought by nonviolent means to induce the al-Hamdi government to move more positively to loosen ties with Saudi Arabia, curb the influence of tribal chiefs, and open up the political system to popular participation.

The NDF now moved toward more militant tactics by smuggling arms and ammunition (reportedly furnished by Libya and other revolutionary Arab states as well as by the PDRY) and by infiltrating guerrillas to challenge the Sanaa government's authority. The latter, in December 1978, sent troops to restore control over some villages near the border. Localized clashes escalated into war between the regular armed forces of the YAR and the PDRY in February 1979. Not surprisingly, each accused the other of initiating the hostilities. After several weeks of fighting, in which the better-equipped PDRY forces occupied three North Yemeni towns with the help of NDF insurgents, acquiescence in a cease-fire was achieved on March 23, 1979, through the efforts of Syria and Iraq (which had momentarily submerged their differences for the sake of common action against the Egyptian-Israeli peace treaty). A few days later the foreign ministers of all the Arab states (except Egypt) met in Kuwait and secured from both Yemeni belligerents agreement to a peace plan providing for the withdrawal of troops, restoration of economic exchanges, and resumption of unity negotiations. Arab League committees were appointed to monitor implementation of the accord and to police the border.

As inter-Yemeni tension rose, the United States had moved naval units into the Arabian Sea, drawing South Yemeni charges of "aggression" and "intervention." Also, a small U.S. arms-supply program for the YAR was sharply expanded and accelerated. As the Saudis were financing the program, however, the United States agreed to ship the equipment, which included armor and aircraft, to Saudi Arabia for assembly and eventual delivery, thus giving Saudi Arabia powerful leverage over North Yemen's policies and actions.

Disarray within the Arab League (the expulsion of Egypt, removal of the league headquarters from Cairo to Tunis, the collapse of the Syria-Iraq rapprochement resulting from their contrasting attitudes toward the Iranian revolution, and so on) limited the effectiveness of its mediation, and sporadic border incidents continued to occur between the two Yemens.

Domestic developments on both sides, however, intervened to produce an improved atmosphere. In North Yemen, the Ali Abdullah Salih regime experimented with a conciliatory policy toward its NDF opposition, conducting discussions with NDF leaders on their possible participation in the government and the holding of national elections. Meanwhile, the preponderant Saudi influence was lessened when the YAR arranged for the supply of weapons from the USSR on long-term credit. In South Yemen, the deposition of Abdul Fattah Ismail as head of state and party chairman in April 1980 was followed by a somewhat more circumspect posture toward the promotion of revolution in the YAR, as well as by a more flexible policy in dealing with the PDRY's other conservative neighbors. The PDRY and YAR presidents had already met in October 1979 in Kuwait and apparently agreed to set aside the Arab League objective of an early and total merger in favor of more realistic goals, including the restoration and expansion of commercial exchanges, travel, and a general normalization of relations. By the fall of 1981, however, the new approach had run its course; the border districts of the YAR were in a state of insurgency led by the NDF with the full support of South Yemen.

THE SULTANATE OF OMAN

At South Yemen's independence, the reactionary sultan of Oman, Sa^cid bin Taymur, was already beset by rebellion in his southern province of Dhofar, bordering on the former Eastern Aden Protectorate. The insurgent organization, the Popular Front for the Liberation of Oman (PFLO),[3] like the NLF, was an offshoot of the Arab Nationalist Movement. To the consequent ideological affinity for the rebels, from the South Yemeni regime's viewpoint, was added the sultan's intimate ties with the United Kingdom based on cordial treaty relations dating from the early nineteenth century. Oman's armed forces and police were staffed by British officers, the United Kingdom handled much of this reclusive country's limited external relations, and the British Royal Air Force had regular use of logistical facilities on its territory. South Yemen gave wholehearted support to the PFLO and covering fire for its guerrilla incursions across the border from South Yemen into Oman, provided sanctuary, served as a channel for the supply of weapons and training by the Soviet bloc and radical Arab states, and placed propaganda services at the PFLO's disposal.

The resulting hostility between South Yemen and Oman was not affected by the Omani coup of July 1970, when Sultan Sa^cid was deposed by his son, Qaboos. For three years, the sultanate had been exporting oil in modest quantities. Whereas his father had simply hoarded the revenues, Qaboos embarked on an intensive program to develop social services—schools, health services, housing, employment, and so on—the lack of which had encouraged disaffection. The new sultan cultivated cooperative relations with the neighboring monarchies, Iran and Saudi Arabia, from whom his father had held aloof. Iran, vitally concerned for the security of the Strait of Hormuz, provided a contingent of troops to assist in combating the rebels, while the Saudis assisted in financing the modernization of the Omani armed forces. These measures drew bitter condemnation from the South Yemenis, whose unflagging support of the PFLO was specifically declared in the ruling party's program approved by the Unification Congress of 1975. Nevertheless, by the end of 1976 the Omani government felt able to announce that the rebellion was at an end, although sporadic exchanges of fire across the border continued to occur between the South Yemeni and Omani regular forces. South Yemen did not abandon its hope of revolution in Oman; on March 25, 1981, the sultan's government filed a memorandum with the Arab League accusing South Yemeni armed forces of committing "acts of aggression" in Dhofar.

Notwithstanding the efforts of Kuwait and other Arab states to effect normalization of relations between Oman and South Yemen, the latter has officially adhered to the principle that it would not enter into diplomatic relations with a country that had foreign troops on its territory. In principle, this obstacle appeared to be removed when the United Kingdom completed the dismantling of its military establishments in Asia and when, after the fall of Shah Muhammad Pahlavi, Iranian forces were withdrawn from Oman. However, Oman's agreement in April 1980 to permit use of its ports and airfields by U.S. armed forces removed any early prospect of a rapprochement. Sultan Qaboos's outspoken view of the pervasive Soviet presence in South Yemen as a serious threat to his own regime and to the general stability of the Arabian Peninsula makes the development of neighborly relations between the two countries an unlikely proposition.

SAUDI ARABIA

The costs in purely practical terms of the South Yemeni regime's orientation are particularly obvious in its relations with its wealthy neighbor to the north, a potential source of massive economic aid. With the sole exception of support for the Palestinian Arab cause there is no common denominator of the two countries' foreign policy objectives and thus no readily apparent basis for the development of friendship and cooperation.

Before South Yemeni independence, contact was quite close between the two regions. Many thousands of South Yemenis lived and worked in the Saudi kingdom. In contrast with the largely unskilled North Yemeni laborers, the Southerners were mostly educated clerks, accountants, or merchants, often of considerable substance – thus, members of the bourgeois class that was to become a casualty of the revolution in their homeland. Saudi relations with the protecting power had been clouded by several territorial disputes in which Britain championed the interests of the states with which it had special treaty arrangements. The Saudis and the British never reached a meeting of minds on the border between the kingdom and the Aden Protectorate. While the British dealt officially with Riyadh on behalf of South Yemen, the Saudi ruling elite maintained cordial informal contact with many of the rulers, themselves aristocrats of traditional outlook.

It will be recalled that the climax of South Yemen's struggle to terminate British rule coincided with the civil war in North Yemen, in which Saudi Arabia and Egypt were arrayed on opposing sides. Hoping to exploit its position in North Yemen to gain control of the future South Yemeni regime, the Egyptians tried to make the NLF their client. This attempt having failed, they sparked the formation of the FLOSY. The

Saudis, well aware that the NLF's orientation was well to the left of Nasserist Arab socialism and unable to support the FLOSY because of its subservience to Egypt, threw their support to the South Arabian League, which had completed its ideological migration from radicalism to conservatism but was failing to win any mass support. The looming prospect of an NLF victory alarmed the Saudis who, despite their differences with the British, endeavored without avail to persuade them to defer their evacuation of South Yemen until the federation could be rendered viable or a moderate element be found to replace foreign rule.

Saudi Arabia long abstained from entering into official relations with the independent South Yemeni regime. Several of the deposed rulers were given asylum in the kingdom and were permitted to seek support from the local representatives of foreign powers, as well as to organize their compatriots in the kingdom for political action. The Corrective Movement in South Yemen brought a flood of refugees. The Saudis observed the leftward march of the PDRY with a growing concern that led them finally to abandon the royalist cause in North Yemen and to sponsor its national reconciliation of March 1970. Thereby, the Saudis hoped to forestall the rise of an aggressively hostile government in Sanaa, but also (as the "guided" Saudi press made quite explicit) to gain an ally for joint military action against the regime in the South.

No serious combined invasion developed, however. In 1971 and 1972 there occurred a few incursions from Saudi Arabia by what South Yemeni official statements termed "mercenaries directed by American officers," but who were in reality South Yemeni irregulars armed by the Saudis and stiffened by a few Saudi army personnel. The Saudis at this time lacked the ability to organize sustained, large-scale military operations in the waterless Empty Quarter where the border region lies, and the South Yemenis had little difficulty in repelling the attacks.

Patient efforts by Kuwait and the Arab League to mediate between the Saudis and South Yemenis bore fruit in 1976, when the rigid policy of the late King Faisal toward the PDRY was relaxed somewhat by his successors, King Khalid and Crown Prince Fahd, who sought a general lessening of inter-Arab tensions. In March of that year, Saudi Arabia extended US$100 million in grant aid to South Yemen. After a tour of the Gulf states by South Yemeni Foreign Minister Muhammad Muti', a project was announced whereby a pipeline would be constructed to carry crude oil from Kuwait, Saudi Arabia, Qatar, and the United Arab Emirates to a loading terminal on the South Yemeni coast, thus providing an alternative route to the vulnerable Strait of Hormuz for the export of these countries' petroleum. In May, formal diplomatic relations were opened for the first time between South Yemen and Saudi Arabia.

The Saudis, however, appear to have moved with too little finesse toward their ultimate objective of maneuvering South Yemen toward a moderate orientation. President Salim Rubayᶜ Ali's forthcoming posture toward the Saudis, as well as his use of a part of their aid to enhance his personal popularity, was among the sources of friction between him and his rivals in the ruling party. Whether he or they carried out the assassination of the North Yemeni president, al-Ghashmi, his opponents were able to exploit the incident by deposing and executing him in June 1978. With his fall the rapprochement with Saudi Arabia came to an end, although relations were not completely severed.

Many aspects of South Yemen's internal policies, such as the nationalization of private property and the public employment of women, are anathema to the Saudi regime as inconsistent with Islam, and the entrenched Soviet position in South Yemen is perceived as a menace to regional security and stability as well as to the life expectancy of the ruling dynasty. For their part, the South Yemenis regard the nature of the Saudi regime, and its close ties with the United States and other Western countries, with undisguised distaste.

Recent Saudi policy has persevered in the effort to reduce tension among the Arabian Peninsula states and to work for coordinated policies and actions. While the response from South Yemen has been minimal, the Saudis have not reverted to their former policy of active hostility and punitive actions, such as preventing bank transfers by South Yemeni workers in the kingdom and refusing to supply crude oil to the Aden refinery. There thus appears to be some possibility that the friction inevitable between the two countries can be kept within manageable bounds.

REGIONAL RELATIONS

Admitted to the Arab League upon independence, South Yemen naturally found association with the more radical group of Arab states more congenial than with its immediate neighbors. Although it has consistently acted as a staunch member of the "rejectionist front" on Arab-Israel issues, its ideology (notwithstanding the advertising of conventional Arab nationalist slogans) subordinates pan-Arabism to solidarity with the global proletariat. The revolutionary Arab states initially regarded South Yemen as a recruit. Iraq, for example, at first actively cultivated the new regime. Four South Yemeni ministers paid an extended visit to Iraq in 1972. Two years later the Iraqi government extended a US$4 million interest-free loan to South Yemen. The latter nevertheless openly castigated the Iraq-Iran treaty of the same year, concluded at a time when it was engaged with Iranian forces in Oman. Iraq, however, seeks to assert leadership of the Arab world by its ruling Baath party faction, which has repressed the Iraqi communists. The South

Yemeni Baathists are a component of the Yemeni Socialist party, but they are quite independent of Iraqi policy. Relations between the two governments deteriorated sharply in June 1979, when an Iraqi "hit squad" murdered an Iraqi communist professor in Aden. Yemeni security forces seized the Iraqi embassy, where the killers had taken refuge; the Iraqi ambassador was recalled.

Algeria has extended technical assistance to South Yemen in the field of oil exploration and continues to encourage its search for a basis of union with North Yemen. Libya has been reported to have financed and deposited stocks of arms in South Yemen intended for use in subverting conservative regimes in the area. South Yemen feels a special rapport with Syria, which also relies heavily on the Soviet Union and which furnished a contingent of several hundred soldiers for the Syrian-dominated Arab peacekeeping force during the Lebanese civil war.

After the Popular Front for the Liberation of the Arab Gulf separated from the Omani dissident movement, South Yemen no longer served as the principal base for subversion of the small Gulf states, with which it maintains some cooperative relations despite differences in political orientation and the absence of resident diplomatic representation. Kuwait, whose admirably managed Fund for Arab Economic Development has well served its purpose as a lightning rod for the designs of more powerful and jealous neighbors, has provided valuable assistance to South Yemen. The latter's independence predated that of Bahrain, Qatar, and the United Arab Emirates (UAE), which assumed full responsibility for their own affairs almost reluctantly and preserve close ties with Britain. The leisurely removal of the British military presence from Bahrain, and the continuance there for several years of a small U.S. naval headquarters, were particularly distasteful to the South Yemenis who, deeming that the initiative belonged to them, opened diplomatic relations with these three states only in 1975, four years after their independence. Relations have been correct, if not close, and the UAE, following the Kuwaiti precedent in the economic field, has extended some assistance to South Yemen.

South Yemen's policy in the Horn of Africa and the Red Sea has paralleled that of the USSR. For a number of years it supported Somali irredentism in the Ogaden and the Eritrean liberation movement. In March 1977 President Salim Rubay^c Ali met at Taiz, in North Yemen, with the Somali, Sudanese, and North Yemeni chiefs of state to consider means of consolidating Arab solidarity "in order to confront Israel's aggressive policy and the Zionist forces supporting it" – an approach in harmony with a general Arab aim of making the Red Sea an Arab lake and ensuring Arab control of its entire littoral. In November of that year, however, the Soviets were evicted from their naval and air installations in Somalia and switched their support to Ethiopia in the conflicts in the Horn. Their facilities were reconsolidated in Aden and Socotra, and South Yemen has served as a key logistical base for Soviet and Cuban military operations in the region, South Yemen thus parting company with most other Arab states respecting the security of the Red Sea basin.

The precedence of the world revolutionary cause over Arab unity and nationalism in the South Yemeni regime's scale of values was confirmed with the signing at Aden in August 1981 of a treaty of friendship and cooperation among the PDRY, Libya, and Ethiopia. Outspokenly aimed at eliminating the U.S. and other Western military presence in the Indian Ocean, Persian Gulf, and Red Sea, the pact sets the three Soviet client states in opposition to Arab League members – Somalia, Egypt, and Oman – that have lent assistance to U.S. strategic planning in the region.

THE SOCIALIST STATES

South Yemen has received significant economic assistance from the World Bank and the International Development Association. It has entered into concessionary arrangements with Japan in the field of fisheries and with Canadian and Dutch firms for petroleum exploration. Beyond the Arab League states and the Horn of Africa, however, its principal preoccupation in the international field has been the cultivation of relations with the socialist community of states.

The importance attached on both sides to this relationship is suggested by the pattern of reciprocal official visits at the chief-of-state or head-of-government level. Thus, during the decade of 1971–1980 the South Yemeni president or premier traveled to Moscow several times, East Germany twice, and at least once each to Hungary, Poland, Czechoslovakia, Romania, Bulgaria, China, North Korea, and Vietnam. Aden received visits by Soviet Premier Kosygin, Fidel Castro, and the Hungarian and East German chiefs of state. During this period no high-level South Yemeni visit was made to any Western country nor to any non-Arab unaligned country.

These relationships have been formalized in intergovernment agreements for economic, financial, technical, and cultural cooperation between South Yemen and the USSR, Romania, the German Democratic Republic, Hungary, and the People's Republic of China. Although the total aid contemplated in these agreements is relatively modest, it may be observed that the paucity of South Yemen's resources limits its economy's ability to put large amounts of capital to productive use.

A certain division of labor may be discerned in the Eastern bloc's activities in South Yemen. The East Germans have long provided assistance in the organization and operation of the country's security and intelligence services, which are an effective deterrent to overt opposition to the ruling party. Cubans have been the source of training for the militia and air force, in addition to furnishing some technical aid, notably in the field of poultry raising. China has engaged in road construction and textile manufacturing, although its activity has diminished since the Maoist-tinged Salim Rubay^c Ali faction lost out definitively in its struggle with supporters of the Soviet model of socialism.

The USSR's influence is, of course, the most pervasive. South Yemen's armed forces are supplied almost exclusively with Soviet arms. The training of party and civil service cadres has been accomplished largely with Soviet advice and help, whether locally or in the Soviet Union. Soviet advice has been sought and received at each major step in the organization of party and government. In the economic field, a joint Soviet-Yemeni fishing venture is in operation, and Soviet technicians have built or improved several irrigation works. USSR political support at the international level has been exceedingly forthcoming. On several occasions the Soviets have declared that they would oppose any armed action against South Yemen, such as the Egyptian notion, during the 1973 war with Israel, of occupying Perim Island in order to deny use of the Red Sea to shipping to and from Israel, or again during the 1979 hostilities with North Yemen. The seal of the relationship was set in October 1979 with the signing of a twenty-year treaty of friendship and cooperation between the two governments. It was followed in November by a similar agreement between South Yemen and East Germany.

The USSR and its satellites reap substantial benefits from their dealings with South Yemen. In addition to rhetorical support for their positions on international issues, they enjoy valuable facilities for the pursuit of their strategic objectives. The floating drydock formerly stationed at Berbera is now at Aden, available for the repair and maintenance of the Soviet Indian Ocean fleet. Access to the local airfields and storage facilities is unrestricted. Tactical use has been made of South Yemen's offshore islands, although reports of the presence of Soviet submarine pens on Socotra have not been confirmed beyond question. Because of the character of the local regime, these activities are, conveniently, largely inaccessible to observation by hostile intelligence services. Whether these arrangements are to be termed military bases is a semantic question it would be idle to discuss here. What is certain is that the USSR has assets in South Yemen worth considerable effort to preserve. Without necessarily accepting the view of some South Yemeni exiles that their country has passed behind the iron curtain, one may reasonably assume that it would be difficult for the country to loosen the Soviet embrace and embark on radically different domestic and foreign policies.

NOTES

1. *Programme of the Unified Political Organisation, the National Front, for the National Democratic Phase of the Revolution* (Nottingham: Russell Press for the PDRY Embassy, London, 1977), pp. 34–36.

2. Absent were Syria, Libya, Algeria, Iraq, the PDRY, and the PLO, all of which had boycotted league activities since the previous December in protest against President Anwar al-Sadat's initiative toward peace with Israel. Djibouti also abstained, presumably because of its delicate situation respecting South Yemen's support of Ethiopia in its dispute with Somalia.

3. Originally the Popular Front for the Liberation of Oman and the Arab Gulf, the movement later split, the Gulf wing becoming a separate organization headquartered in Bahrain.

Suggested Further Reading

As the present work is addressed more to the general Western reader than to the area specialist, the publications recommended here are largely confined to those in Western languages and accessible without undue difficulty in, or through, the larger libraries.

No significant natural, ethnic, or cultural feature set South Yemen apart from the rest of "geographic" Yemen until the Ottoman and British Empires asserted their respective control of the two regions in the nineteenth century. The Hadramawt sayyids and the Zaidi imams did, indeed, have their distinct chronicles, only partially overlapping. By and large, however, it was South Yemen's experience under foreign, non-Muslim rule that fostered the present national personality contrasting with that of its northern neighbor. Information on South Yemen before 1839, thus, is to be sought primarily in works dealing with Southern Arabia as a whole.

Much archaeological spadework remains to be done before a comprehensive account of pre-Islamic Yemen can be written. Complicating the task of describing ancient Yemeni society and tracing its history is the fact that, with the economic decline of the area after the first century A.D., the local inscriptions (the only surviving indigenous records) became quite sparse, and knowledge of the old *musnad* script decreased along with that of the ancient South Arabic language in which the inscriptions were expressed. As a result, documented knowledge of their earliest history died out among the Yemeni people. By the ninth century, when Arabs began writing history, the entire pre-Islamic era in South Arabia was known to them as the era of the Himyarites, who united Yemen under a single government as late as the third century A.D., and their accounts of the remote periods are encrusted with a thick layer of legend and invention.

The Western science of archaeology arose only in the nineteenth century. Scholars have collected and interpreted an impressive body of *musnad* inscriptions and collated them with accounts by classical Greek and Latin writers. Excavation, on the other hand, has been conducted at very few Yemeni sites. Among these is the "dig" in Wadi ʿAmd by Gertrude Caton Thompson, published in *The Tombs and Moon Temple of Hureidha (Hadramaut)* (Oxford: Oxford University Press, 1944). The American Foundation for the Study of Man expedition of 1950–1952 excavated in Wadi Bayhan and at Marib, across the border in North Yemen. The formal report of the work is *Archaeological Discoveries in South*

Arabia (Baltimore: Johns Hopkins Press, 1958), by Richard LeBaron Bowen, Jr., and Frank P. Albright, which contains an absorbing description of ancient agriculture in the kingdom of Qataban, a discussion of ancient Yemeni trade routes, and material on other aspects of ancient Yemen. On a less technical level, *Qataban and Sheba* (London: Victor Gollancz, 1955), by Wendell Phillips, the foundation's president, gives a popular account of the expedition's work and conclusions.

The pitfalls involved in sorting out truth and error in remote Yemeni history are well illustrated by *Sheba's Daughters—Being a Record of Travel in Southern Arabia* (London: Methuen, 1939) by that indefatigable explorer of Arabia and hanger-on of the Saudi Arabian court, H.St.J.B. Philby, who visited a number of archaeological sites in South Yemen. Philby's mistaken assumptions regarding the chronology of the ancient states beguiled him into fanciful conclusions pushing back the dawn of Yemeni civilization beyond that in Egypt and Mesopotamia. These notions were later embraced by Yemeni writers who have disregarded the more rigorous analysis of the available evidence presented in Jacqueline Pirenne's *Le Royaume Sud-Arabe de Qataban et sa datation* [The South Arabian Kingdom of Qataban and its dates] (Louvain: Publications Universitaires, 1961). Mlle. Pirenne's teacher, Jacques Ryckmans, gave an exhaustive study of the *musnad* material available at time of his writing in *L'Institution monarchique en Arabie méridionale avant l'Islam* [The pre-Islamic institution of monarchy in Southern Arabia] (Louvain: Publications Universitaires, 1951). Given the insufficient groundwork, no Western scholar has undertaken the sort of broad synthesis on ancient Yemen attempted in Jawad Ali's seven-volume *Al-ʿArab Qabl al-Islam* [The Arabs before Islam] (Baghdad: Matbaʿat al-Tafayyud al-Ahliya, 1952). For the time being, the reader seeking detailed information on pre-Islamic Yemen beyond the few published books must turn to occasional articles in such periodicals as *Antiquity, Geographical Journal, Arabica, Journal of the Royal Geographical Society, Bulletin of the American Schools of Oriental Research, Oriente Moderno,* and *Journal of the Royal Asiatic Society.*

Upon conversion of the Arabian Peninsula to Islam in the seventh century, South Yemen became an integral part of the expanding Islamic state. While Yemenis were full participants in the building of the empire they were (with the exception of the small Jewish community) mostly illiterate, and no indigenous records of local events in the early Islamic era survive. Such knowledge as exists is confined to occasional observations by the new school of historians centered far to the north, whose attention was concentrated on Syria and Mesopotamia, where the decisive historical issues were being decided. Literacy in the standard Koranic Arabic was introduced very gradually into South Yemen by missionaries seeking to instruct the people in the duties of the new faith. Not until the tenth century did a literate South Yemeni class begin to form under the leadership of immigrant descendants of the Prophet, in whose hands education remained until the twentieth century and who wrote annals of local events of which some survive in Arabic manuscript. Informative in this connection is Robert B. Serjeant's *The Saiyids of Hadramawt* (London: School of Oriental and African Studies, 1957).

Aside from the Hadrami chronicles, difficult of access, enlightenment on South Yemen through the fifteenth century must be sought in works dealing with the medieval states centered at Zabid, Sanaa, and Taiz, whose territory often included the South. Among the more instructive works available in English are Shaikh Hasan bin Ali al-Khazraji's *The Pearl-Strings: A History of the Resuliy Dynasty of Yemen,* in J. W. Redhouse's quaint translation (London: Luzac, 1906–1907), and the Henry Cassels Kay translation of Umara al-Yamani's history, *Yaman—Its Early Medieval History* (London: Edward Arnold, 1892). The former offers valuable information on the commercial traffic through the port of Aden under the Rasulids; further details can be found in Robert B. Serjeant and Claude Cahen, "A Fiscal Survey of the Medieval Yemen," *Arabica,* Vol. 4, no. 1 (1957): 23–30.

For the momentous European penetration of the Indian Ocean basin beginning at the close of the fifteenth century, Robert B. Serjeant's *The Portuguese off the South Arabian Coast* (Oxford: Clarendon Press, 1963) is highly recommended; the work draws both upon contemporary European writings and upon manuscript chronicles from Hadramawt. The Portuguese incursion touched off the series of events in which areas of South Yemen were conquered by Egyptian Mamelukes, became part of the Ottoman Province of Yemen, were occupied briefly by the resurgent Zaidis, then fragmented into numerous autonomous statelets until 1839, when the British landed in Aden and began their slow penetration of the interior.

A broad overview of the British presence in South Yemen is provided in R. J. Gavin's *Aden Under British Rule 1839–1967* (London: C. Hurst, 1975). This volume suggests an alarming decline in England of the humble art of proof-reading. (In one passage, what should obviously read "Qu‘aiti" appears as "Kuwaiti"! Other such whoppers are all too frequent.) The book is nevertheless meticulously researched in the British and India Office archives and the general published literature. Particularly informative on the formation of British imperial policy toward South Yemen, it also offers many insights into the local society, politics, and economy. A useful bibliography is included.

Establishment of the Aden colony inaugurated the era of Western travel in South Yemen and publication of first-hand observations, whether by colonial officials or laymen, often sensitive observers and competent writers. The following books are recommended as offering reliable descriptions at intervals during British rule. The first systematic, carefully researched work is Capt. Frederick M. Hunter's *Account of the British Settlement of Aden in Arabia* (London, 1877; deservedly reprinted in 1968 by Frank Cass & Co., London). Prepared for the government of India's Statistical Department, it provides detailed data on the colony's geography, population, trade, navigation, communications, administration, and local customs as of the early 1870s. If Hunter's description of the hinterland is weak, it may be recalled that solid, first-hand British knowledge had not yet progressed beyond Aden's immediate neighbors. The remoter parts of the Western Protectorate are the subject of *The Land of Uz* (London: St. Martin's, 1911) by G. Wyman Bury, an Aden political officer during the abortive "forward policy" period after the turn of the twentieth century. Bury (who adopted the name "Abdullah Mansur" when traveling locally) aimed his colorful work at the general public, but offered a wealth of information on the tribes, their way of life, and their geographical setting. For the area's politics at the same period, the pertinent sections of Robin Bidwell's *Affairs of Arabia 1905–1906* (London: Frank Cass & Co., 1971, 2 vols.) are authoritative.

Several Western visitors to South Yemen during the 1920s and 1930s published valuable descriptions. Among these may be mentioned Bertram Thomas's *Arabia Felix* (London: J. Cape, 1932) and Freya Stark's *Southern Gates of Arabia* (London: John Murray, 1936). The Dutch diplomat and Arabist, Daniel van der Meulen, made two productive trips to Hadramawt, drawn by the close links between that area and the large Hadrami community in the Dutch East Indies. The first, in 1931, made in the company of the German scholar H. von Wissman, occurred during a period of great civil unrest but resulted in much acute observation and the first reliable published map of the Eastern Protectorate (*Hadramaut: Some of its Mysteries Unveiled* [Leyden: E. J. Brill, 1964]). Van der Meulen's second journey took place in 1939, when the political resident, W. H. Ingrams, was orchestrating his intertribal peace; the later account makes a revealing contrast with the earlier one (*Aden to the Hadhramaut: A Journey in South Arabia*, London: John Murray, 1947). Ingrams himself wrote an insightful description in *Arabia and the Isles* (London, 1942; 2nd ed., John Murray, 1966), and his wife, D. S. Ingrams, an informative work in her *Survey of the Economic and Social Conditions in the Aden Protectorate* (Asmara: Government Printer, British Administration, 1949).

Several of the later British governors of South Yemen wrote accounts of their stewardship, and these are of obvious interest and importance. The first, and abortive, British efforts to unite the country politically were made during the tenure of Sir Tom Hickinbotham, whose memoirs appear in *Aden* (London: Constable, 1958). Sir Charles Johnston – *The View from Steamer Point* (New York: Frederick A. Praeger, 1964) – held the post at the time of the North Yemeni revolution of 1962, with its important repercussions in the South. By far the most interesting for its acute and sympathetic insight into the mentality of the South Yemenis is *Shades of Amber: A South Arabian Episode* (London: Hutchinson, 1968) by Sir Kennedy Trevaskis, the principal architect of the South Arabian Federation, who had spent most of his long colonial service career in South Yemen.

Two works by South Yemenis dealing with their country on the eve of independence deserve attention. *L'Evolution politique, économique et sociale de L'Arabie du Sud* [The political, economic, and social evolution of South Arabia] (Algiers: Société Nationale d'Edition et de Diffusion, 1966), by Muhammad ꞌUmar al-Habashi, smacks of the unpruned doctoral thesis. Its inept effort to apply to a colonial regime criteria more suitable to the administration of an independent country results in gratuitous criticism of British policy, and its extended "advice to princes" discussion of how best to manage South Yemen's oil resources has been rendered pointless by the failure to discover any. The work nevertheless gives a useful compendium of the available economic and social data on the eve of independence and provides illuminating comments on various social and political aspects of the society. Of greater significance is Abdalla S. Bujra, *The Politics of Stratification: A Study of Political Change in a South Arabian Town* (Oxford: Oxford University Press, 1971), a penetrating study of a single Hadrami town (Hurayda) by an able political scientist. While its conclusions should not be extrapolated indiscriminately to the whole of South Yemen, the book is indispensable to an understanding of the sources of the country's revolution and of the course its politics have taken.

Regrettably little material on independent South Yemen is available in Western languages (and not much reliable information even in Arabic); as the society is closed to scholarly investigation, this situation is not likely soon to change. The survey conducted by the World Bank in 1977 had the full cooperation of the South Yemeni authorities. The admirable resulting report, *People's Democratic Republic of Yemen: A Review of Economic and Social Development* (Washington, D.C.), published by the bank in 1979, is invaluable as a detailed description of the country's economy after a decade or so of revolution. For a more general, and more political, perspective, by far the best analyses available are by Fred Halliday: Part Three of his *Arabia Without Sultans* ([New York: Vintage, 1975], pp. 165–274) and "Yemen's Unfinished Revolution: Socialism in the South" (Middle East Research and Information Project, October 1979, pp. 3–20). Although this author's writing is not devoid of the reification and questionable assumptions often encountered in current leftist thought, it rests on a solid body of information, much of it acquired at first hand, that is to be found nowhere else.

Abbreviations

ANM	Arab Nationalist Movement
ATUC	Aden Trades Union Congress
BP	British Petroleum
FLOSY	Front for the Liberation of Occupied South Yemen
GDP	Gross domestic product
GUYW	General Union of Yemeni Women
NDF	National Democratic Front
NLF	National Liberation Front
PDFLP	People's Democratic Front for the Liberation of Palestine
PDRY	People's Democratic Republic of Yemen
PFLO	Popular Front for the Liberation of Oman
PLO	Palestine Liberation Organization
PSP	People's Socialist Party
RAF	Royal Air Force
SAL	South Arabian League
UAE	United Arab Emirates
UNESCO	United Nations Educational, Scientific and Cultural Organization
YAR	Yemen Arab Republic

Index

Abbas, 24

Abbasids, 21, 22, 23, 24, 73

Abdali sultans, 37, 40, 70, 77

Abdul Fattah Ismail, 62, 64, 65, 66, 68, 69, 72(n6), 97, 98

Abdullah Abd al-Alim, 96

Abdullah bin Zubayr, 21

Abdul Qawi Makkawi, 62–63

Abraha, 19, 20

Abu Bakr (caliph), 20

Abyan Development Board, 51, 78–79

Abyan district, 74, 78–79

Aden, 17, 23, 25, 27, 28–29, 73, 74, 104

British occupation of, 30, 31–45, 50, 51, 56, 75–80, 91–92

fortification of, 33, 75–76

and Lahej, 37, 39

Legislative Council, 35–36, 55

modernization of, 33–35

and Ottoman Turks, 29, 42

population of, 33, 35, 36

port. See also Shipping

and South Arabian Federation, 55

Aden Association, 36

Aden Protectorate Levies, 42, 45, 54

Aden refinery, 84–85, 102. See also British Petroleum refinery

Aden Trades Union Congress (ATUC), 55, 56, 61, 62

Adnan, 3, 6

Africa, 41, 76, 103, 104

Agriculture, 2, 10, 17, 73, 74, 81–83, 92

under British occupation, 44, 51, 77, 78–79

cropping patterns, 82–83

in Eastern Protectorate, 79

in Lahej, 79

nationalization of, 81, 82–83

and personal income, 88

productivity, 82–83(table 1)

under Rasulids, 26

in Wadi Bana, 78

Ahmad bin Abdullah (sultan), 63

Ahmad bin Sulaiman (imam), 24

Ahmad Mukhtar, 39

Aidrus Muhammad, 51–52

Akhdam, 8–9, 13

Aksum, 18–19

Alawi, 40, 41, 42

Albuquerque (admiral), 29

Alexander the Great, 18

Algeria, 95, 96, 103, 106(n2)

Ali Abd al-ᶜAlim, 72(n6)

Ali Abdullah Salih, 97, 98

Ali antar, 62, 72(n6)

Ali bin Abd al-Karim, 53–54

Ali bin Abi Talib, 6, 20–21

Ali bin al-Fadl, 23

Ali bin Maᶜn, 23

Ali Nasser Muhammad al-Hasani, 66, 69, 96

Anatolia, 31

ANM. See Arab Nationalist Movement

Anticolonialism. See Arab nationalism

Aqrabi state, 39, 40, 79

115

Painting, 13
Palestine Liberation Organization
(PLO), 93, 106(n2)
Palmerston, Lord, 32
Pan-Arabism. *See* Arab unity
PDFLP. *See* People's Democratic
Front for the Liberation of
Palestine
People's Democratic Front for the
Liberation of Palestine (PDFLP),
60–61
People's Democratic Union, 68
"People's guards," 64, 66
People's Local Councils, 70–71
People's Republic of China, 84, 104,
105. *See also* China
People's Socialist party (PSP), 55, 61,
62
People's Supreme Council, 70, 71
Perim Island, 30, 77
Personal income, 88–90
Petroleum Board, 81
PFLO. *See* Popular Front for the
Liberation of Oman
PLO. *See* Palestine Liberation
Organization
Poetry, 12–13
Poland, 104
"Popular democratic liberation,"
64, 66
Popular Front for the Liberation of
Oman (PFLO), 99
Popular Front for the Liberation of
Oman and the Arab Gulf,
106(n3)
Popular Front for the Liberation of
the Arab Gulf, 103
Population, 89(table 3). *See also*
Aden, population of; Demo-
graphics
Porte, 29, 39, 40, 41, 47
Ports Board, 81
Port Trust, 77
Portugal, 28–29, 30, 74
Poverty, 87, 88
Presidium, 66, 69, 70
Productivity, 82–83(table 1), 92.

See also Economy
Protectorate Levies. *See* Aden
Protectorate Levies
PSP. *See* People's Socialist party

Qaboos, 99, 100
Qahtan, 3, 4
Qansuh al-Ghawri, 29
Qasimis, 30
Qataban, 17, 18
Qatar, 101, 103
Qishn, 50
al-Quᶜaiti, Umar bin Awad, 47
Quᶜaiti-Kathiri war, 47
Quᶜaiti state, 8, 50, 55, 59
Quraysh, 6, 27
Qutaybi, 8

RAF. *See* Royal Air Force
Rainfall. *See* Climate
Raᶜiya, 8
Rangelands, 81–82. *See also*
Agriculture
al-Rashid, Haroun, 21
al-Rasul, Nur al-Din Umar bin Ali,
25–26
Rasulids, 25–28, 74
Raw Cotton Commission (Br.), 78,
79
Regional relations, 102–104
Retail trade
nationalization of, 81
Romania, 104
Royal Air Force (RAF), 42–43, 48,
76, 99
al-Ruᶜayni, Ali bin Mahdi, 24

Saba, 17–18
Sabi. See Subyan
Sacred enclave. *See Hawta*
al-Sadat, Anwar, 106(n2)
al-Sadiq, Jaᶜfar (imam), 22
Saᶜid bin Taymur, 99
SAL. *See* South Arabian League
Saladin (sultan of Egypt), 25
Salih (sultan), 48
Salih Muslih, 72(n6)

DATE DUE

JUL 9 '85			
OCT 13 '88 S			
NOV 1 9 '92 S			